SIMPLE RULES
for Card Games

ACKNOWLEDGMENTS

Special thanks to: Blue Highway Games, Matt Morgan, Jordan Rubin, Susan Mitchell, Christina Vaule, Mike Stahl, Susan Stahl, Monique Vescia, Scott Siler, Leisa Goldberg, Bob Christopher, and Matt Bien. And to Charles and Charlotte Rauf, who got me hooked on card games at a very young age.

ISBN 978-0-385-36557-4

Printed in China

www.potterstyle.com

Design by Jenny Kraemer

10 9 8 7 6 5 4 3 2 1

Special Edition

SIMPLE RULES
for Card Games

———◆———

Instructions and Strategy
for Twenty Card Games

———◆———

WRITTEN BY DON RAUF

POTTER STYLE
New York

CONTENTS

Introduction **6**
Glossary of Basic Terms **7**

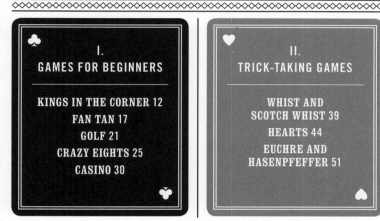

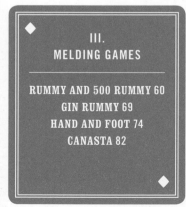

Card Game Cocktails **127**

♣ INTRODUCTION ♠

Knowing how to play card games is a social skill, on par with being able to tell jokes and make easy conversation. Playing cards is a great way to engage and interact with all kinds of people—acquaintances, good friends, and family alike. The strain of small talk lifts when everyone is focused on their hands. A card game also provides ample opportunity for banter.

Learning how to play card games, however, can be intimidating. Rule books are dense with jargon, online tutorials move too fast, and your uncle just doesn't have the patience for beginners.

Presented in a clear, step-by-step fashion, the instructions in this book represent the simplest way to play twenty highly popular card games. Complicated penalty rules and some convoluted features have been edited out of these instructions, but the essence of each game—and what makes it fun—remains intact.

For the true novice, the games in the first chapter are a good place to start. The games in subsequent chapters are organized progressively, so that the skills you pick up from one game carry over to a more challenging one.

Simply put, having a few card games in your back pocket will make you feel smart and accomplished.

♥ GLOSSARY OF ◆ BASIC TERMS

Throughout this book, card-playing terms are defined on the spot and the text is generally jargon-free. If you are completely new to card playing, it is helpful to become familiar with this basic list of terms (especially the two definitions for the word "hand"). Initially, expressions like "taking the trick" will sound foreign, but you will start to enjoy using real card-playing terminology with time.

BID	A bid is the number of tricks that you *think* you can win before playing a hand. Many games require you to make your best guess, based on the hand you've been dealt.
BUILD	Placing cards together to form a unique grouping. For example, in Casino, a 6 can be placed on a 3 to *build* 9s. In Solitaire, players form builds of cards by alternating in color and descending order.
DEAL	Distributing cards to all of the players, according to the rules of the game.
DISCARD	Removing a card from your hand is often called *discarding*; the discarded card itself is often called a *discard*.

DISCARD PILE | The pile where players stack cards eliminated from their hands over the course of the game.

ELDEST HAND | The player to the left of the dealer; depending on the game, this player is often required to make the opening bid or play the first card.

FOLLOW SUIT | When playing a trick-taking game (see *Trick* below), following suit means playing a card from your hand that matches the suit of the lead card.

GO OUT | Playing the last card in your hand is called *going out*. In many cases, the winner of the game is the player who goes out first.

HAND | This term has two common uses: (1) It refers to the cards that have been dealt to each player (i.e., the cards that have been dealt to you are your hand). (2) A hand is also one "round" of play, comprised of trick-taking, melding, building, or any activity specific to the game, until at least one player has played all of the cards in his or her hand. A hand concludes when scores are tallied and the cards are gathered and shuffled. The next hand begins when the cards are dealt again. Most games consist of several hands.

MELD | A combination or group of cards that score points, depending on the rules of the game. *Melding* is the act of pairing or combining cards to form melds.

OPEN

In bidding games, opening means making your first bet or bid. In melding games, opening means putting your first meld down on the table.

POT

In gambling games, the pot is the amount of money or chips in the center of the table. It is awarded to the winner of the hand.

RANK

The value of the card. Standard card ranking (high to low) is A, K, Q, J, 10, 9, 8, 7, 6, 5, 4, 3, 2.

RUN

A sequence of three or more cards of the same suit (e.g., K♦, Q♦, J♦).

SEQUENCE

Two or more cards of adjacent rank, but not necessarily in the same suit (e.g., 7♦, 8♣).

STOCK

The pile of cards left over after the players have been dealt their hands, which is often used during the course of the game for drawing additional cards.

SUIT

The four types of cards (suits) are hearts ♥, diamonds ♦, spades ♠, and clubs ♣.

TRICK

A round of play where each participant in succession plays one card from his or her hand, placing it in the center of the table. *Taking a trick* is the expression for winning all of the cards on the table. Typically a player wins the trick when he plays the highest card in the leading suit or the highest trump card.

TRUMP | Any suit that has been elevated (according to the rules of the individual game) to a more powerful status than the other three suits.

WILD CARD | A card that can be any rank or suit, as declared by the holder (e.g., in Canasta the Joker is a wild card, so if player wants to form a three-card meld with the Q♦ and Q♠, the Joker can be used in the place of a queen).

I

If you haven't played a card game since Go Fish, start with the selections in this chapter. Although the rules are simple (especially Kings in the Corner, which is essentially a social version of Solitaire), these games won't insult your intelligence. After a few hands, you'll graduate to a more strategic way of playing. Casino, admittedly, has lots of rules and should not be attempted first.

KINGS IN THE CORNER, 2–6 PLAYERS

FAN TAN, 3–8 PLAYERS

GOLF, 2–4 PLAYERS

CRAZY EIGHTS, 2–12 PLAYERS

CASINO, 2–4 PLAYERS

KINGS IN THE CORNER

A SOLITAIRE-LIKE GAME FOR MORE THAN ONE PLAYER

This game follows the principles of Solitaire, except that you play with others. Some say it was created in 1910 by passengers on the SS *Suvic* (a steamship that traveled between England and Australia) as a way to pass the time at sea. By the end of the game you have rows of cards, alternating in color, fanning away from the center stockpile. This is an easy game to play and moderately challenging. It's a great warm-up before getting into more sophisticated games.

RATING Very Easy

PLAYERS 2–6 players; 4 is best.

DECK One full deck of 52 cards without the Jokers.

RANKING Standard ranking with king high and ace low.

OBJECTIVE To be the first to get rid of all the cards in your hand.

◇◇

HOW TO PLAY

DEAL THE CARDS. Distribute one card to each player, clockwise, until each player has seven cards. Then put the remaining cards (the stock) facedown in the middle and flip over the next four cards and place them at north, east, south, and west around the deck. The four cards around the stock form the foundation piles for discarding.

PLAY YOUR TURN. The player to the dealer's left (the eldest) takes the first turn. You can perform *any or all* of the following options in one turn:

Set down a single card from your hand on any of the foundation piles. As with Solitaire, your card has to be next lower in rank and the opposite color of the foundation card (lay it down overlapping so you can see the card beneath).

Pick up one of the four foundation piles and overlap it with another foundation pile (again, following the rules of Solitaire). You can move as many piles that will overlap in a single turn. For example, if one pile has 9♥, 8♣, 7♦, and there is a 10♠ as the top card on another foundation pile, you can move the 9♥, 8♣, 7♦ and place it atop the 10♠. Now there will be an empty foundation pile spot and you can fill it with any card from your hand. Any time you can create an empty foundation pile spot, you can fill it with a card from your hand.

You can set down any kings in your hand during a turn. Kings are placed in a diagonal between the foundation cards at points NE, SE, SW, and NW.

EXAMPLE Here is a sample of the series of moves that you can make in one turn.

The foundation cards are as follows:

Suppose you have a 6♣ and a 3♥ in your hand. You must decide which card to play first: you can either lay down the 6♣ on the 7♥ or place the 3♥ on the 4♠, but you cannot play both cards in one turn. You decide to place your 6♣ on the 7♥.

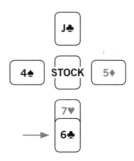

In this same turn, you can move the 4♠ on top of the 5♦, creating an empty foundation spot where the 4♠ was.

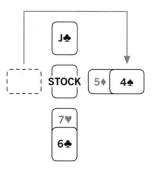

Then you can move the 4♠/5♦ pile on top of the 6♣. By doing this, you create two empty foundation spaces. You can fill these empty spaces with any two cards from your hand. (In this example, a 10♣ and a 9♠.)

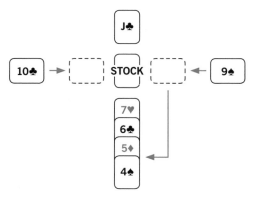

Finally, if you have a king in your hand, you can set it down in any of the four corners to begin new foundation piles. During your turn, you may also lay any eligible cards in your hand on top of the king.

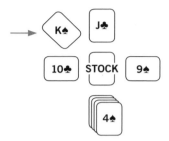

Your turn ends when you've played as many cards from your hand as possible. If you *can't* make any of the moves described above, simply draw a card from stock and add it to your hand (you cannot play this card until your next turn).

Eventually, the pile will wind up radiating diagonally off the kings and away from the stock.

ENDING THE HAND. The first one to place all his or her cards wins. This tends to be a fast-moving game and frequently players go out quickly.

◇◇

SCORING

Generally, players score a point per hand won. You can decide how many hands to play depending on the number of players (best out of three hands wins or best out of five hands, etc.)

FAN TAN

Fan Tan, also known as Sevens, Stops, Domino, and Parliament, is believed to have originated from an ancient Chinese gambling game. Do not confuse this card game with a different Chinese gambling game—resembling roulette—that is also called Fan-Tan (with a hyphen). While gambling can still be an element in this card game, you don't have to gamble to have fun playing. And although it is simple, there can be strategy in how you play. As one online fan of Fan Tan says, "It doesn't matter if you have a horrible hand or an amazing one; what matters is how you play. The best hand can still lose if you can't properly manipulate the players into doing what you want by placing your cards carefully. The worst hand, with a bit of luck and a lot of strategy, can still be turned around for a win."

RATING Very Easy

PLAYERS 3–8 players. Each player plays for himself or herself, not in partnership.

DECK One full deck of 52 cards without Jokers.

RANKING Standard ranking, but with king high to ace low.

OBJECTIVE To be the first to get rid of all the cards in your hand.

<><><><><><><><><><><><><><><><><><><><><><><><><><><><><><><><><><><><><>

HOW TO PLAY

DEAL THE CARDS. Distribute one card to each player, clockwise, until all cards are given out. It's okay if a player gets an extra card.

Play your 7s. The player to the left of the dealer goes first. To start, each player must play a 7 or pass.

Add cards to the 7s. Once a 7 is placed in the middle of the table, the next player can either add a 6 to the left or an 8 to the right of the 7 (the 6 and the 8 must be the same suit as the 7). Alternatively, this player can lay down another 7 to begin a new fan. Each person plays only one card per turn.

EXAMPLE **PLAYER 1** plays the 7♦

PLAYER 2 can either add a 6♦ before the 7, add an 8♦ after the 7, or lay down another 7 in a separate row. Player 2 adds a 6♦.

PLAYER 3 can then either add the 5♦ to the 6, the 8♦ after the 7, or lay down another 7 in a separate row. Player 3 lays down a 7♠.

PLAYER 4 can add onto the 7♠, play the 5♦ or 8♦, or play another 7. **PLAYER 4** lays down 8♦.

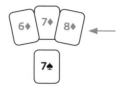

NOTE You're always building lower in sequence to the left of the 7s down to the ace and higher to the right of the 7s up to the king. If you have a card you can play, you must play it.

END THE HAND. Players take turns adding cards to the fans until one person has played all of his cards, winning the game.

SCORING

The first player out of cards wins, but you can extend the game by playing multiple hands. Because the game revolves around 7s, it is fun to play the best of seven games (whoever wins the most rounds wins).

OPTIONAL RULES

If you want to add in a gambling element, players can be given chips (pennies are fine too). You can start with an ante (each player puts a chip into the pot) at the beginning of each hand. If any player is dealt an extra card, he puts in two chips.

When someone wins by playing all of his cards, the remaining players count the cards in their hand; they must each give a chip per card to the pot. The winner then collects the pot.

GOLF

LIKE REAL GOLF, THE LOWEST SCORE WINS

Golf is popular throughout North America, Great Britain, and other English-speaking countries. It is sometimes called Polish Polka and Polish Poker. Some call the four-card version here Turtle. Note that there is a Golf Solitaire game that has nothing to do with this game. People usually play nine or eighteen rounds of this game (matching the number of holes played in the sport).

RATING Very Easy

PLAYERS 2–4 players.

DECK One full deck of 52 cards without Jokers.

RANKING Ranking doesn't matter but point value of cards does.

OBJECTIVE To have the lowest score possible.

SCORING

QUEENS AND JACKS = 10 points each
ACE TO 10 = point value (ace is 1 point, 2 is 2 points, 3 is 3 points, etc.)
KINGS = 0 points each

HOW TO PLAY

DEAL THE CARDS. Dealer gives out four cards per player. Without looking at the cards, the players arrange their hands facedown on the table in a square formation. The remaining deck is placed in the middle. The top card is turned over to start the discard pile.

Assess your hand and discard. After you have arranged your cards in a square, you may peek at your bottom two cards to assess whether you have a low-scoring hand. Starting with the player on the dealer's right, each player has an opportunity to discard a high-scoring card and attempt to replace it with a new card from the stock or the discard pile that might improve her overall score.

PLAYING YOUR TURN. When it is your turn, you can:

Draw a card from the top of the deck (the stock). If you decide to keep this card, you must discard one of your four cards and replace it with the new card (facedown). You can also opt to put this new card immediately in the discard pile, faceup.

Remember, you do not know what your two top cards are unless you decide to discard and replace them. You can see these cards only upon discard, when you place them faceup on the discard pile.

Take the top card on the discard pile. If you think this card will help you get a low score and win, take it and replace one of your four cards with this card. Then discard. Of course, if you take the discard pile card, other players will know what points you are taking in that turn.

If you think you have a winning (lowest) score, you can knock on the table instead of drawing and discarding. After you knock, each player gets to have one more turn to draw and discard. Then all players turn over their four cards, revealing their final scores.

ENDING THE HAND. Once everyone has taken a turn drawing a card and discarding, all players reveal their cards, and whoever has the lowest score wins that hand. The cards are gathered and another hand is dealt. Usually, you play to the best of 9 or 18 rounds.

VARIATION

SIX-CARD GOLF

In this version (sometimes called Hari Kari), players are dealt six cards that they lay facedown in front of them in two rows of three. You do not look at any of the cards but you randomly turn over two of your cards for all players to see.

On your turn, you either draw a card from the top of the deck (the stock) or take the top card of the discard pile and use it to replace any one of your six cards. If you draw from the stock, you have the option of immediately discarding that card if you wish.

When you replace a facedown card with a drawn card, you do not look at the card you are replacing. You will know what it is only upon discard. When you replace a card, you put the new card in its place, faceup, and put the old card faceup on the discard pile.

There is no knocking. All players play until all cards are faceup, and then the hands are scored.

NOTE Ten-Card Golf is played just like Six-Card Golf but you usually use two decks.

CRAZY EIGHTS

A GAME WHERE THE 8 CHANGES THE SUIT

This card-shedding game is also known as Eights and Swedish Rummy. The game is similar to Mau Mau, Switch, Crates, Last One, Rockaway, Tschausepp (in Switzerland), and Pesten (in Norway). Some people play an identical game called Crazy Jacks where the jacks take the wild card role of the 8s. The game belongs to a family of games called "stops" because players can be stopped from discarding if they don't have the appropriate card. Crazy Eights is a well-known children's game, but it's fun for all ages. Some say the game originated in the 1940s when the term "crazy eights" was used to describe a mentally unstable soldier, known as a Section 8.

RATING Easy

PLAYERS 2–12 players.

DECK One full deck without Jokers for up to 6 players; two full decks for 7 to 12 players.

RANKING Ranking is not part of this game.

OBJECTIVE To be the first to get rid of all the cards in your hand.

HOW TO PLAY

DEAL THE CARDS. Distribute one card to each player, clockwise, until each player has five cards. When playing with just two players, deal seven cards to each. After cards are dealt, the remaining deck (the stock) is placed in the middle and the top card is turned over and placed by the side of the deck to start the discard pile. If the first card turned over is an 8, it is placed back in the middle of the deck and the next card is flipped over.

PLAYING YOUR TURN. Starting to the dealer's left, each player has a turn to get rid of a card in his hand. You can discard any card in your hand that matches the number or suit of the card on top of the discard pile.

EXAMPLE **If the top card on the discard pile is Q♣,** you can discard any queen from your hand or any club from your hand. If you discard a Q♥, then the next player can discard any other queen or any heart.

You also can discard an 8 on your turn. 8s are basically wild cards and when you discard one you can name the suit that you want the discard pile to be.

If you have no cards in your hand that you can play, you must draw from the stock until you draw a card that you can discard. If you draw from the stock and exhaust the entire pile, then you must pass.

ENDING THE HAND. Whoever gets rid of all his cards first wins. Then the cards are all returned to the deck and the player to the left of the last dealer deals the next round.

In the rare case that the stock is exhausted and no one can play any cards, then the player holding the least amount of points wins.

◇◇◇

STRATEGY

You may draw cards from the stock even if you have a card you can play, if you find yourself in the following situation:

You are playing against one other person. He has two cards left. He discards an 8 and changes the suit to spades. Now you know that his final card is most likely a spade. You know that all the 8s have not been played, so you decide to draw cards until you get an 8 and can change the suit.

◇◇◇

SCORING

One person keeps score for all players. Some play that you simply get a point for each hand you win. Others play that the winner gets points according to the cards that the other players are holding using this scoring system:

8 = 50 points each
K, Q, J, 10 = 10 points each
A = 1 point each
ALL OTHER CARDS = face value (for example, 4♦ = 4 points)

Adding in creative rules. Since this game is called Crazy Eights, some groups add in their own "crazy" rules. For example, if you play a 10, you have to run around your chair three times. Or if you draw a queen you have to do a shot.

VARIATION

SWITCH

This game is like a very elaborate version of Crazy Eights. You discard cards in the same way, but there are "power cards" that introduce more rules into the game. Here is a common version.

If you play a jack, the direction of play reverses or "switches"—instead of going clockwise, it will now go counterclockwise until someone plays another jack.

If you play a 2, the next person must first draw two cards from the stock and then resume normal play by either discarding a card that matches the 2's suit or continuing to draw cards from the stock until he finds such as card. However, if that person has a 2, he may discard it and the next person must draw four cards and then resume normal play. If that person has a 2, the next person draws 6 and so on.

If you play a 4, the same rules apply but with the next person drawing four cards first, and so on.

If you play an 8, the next player loses a turn, but you can't change the suit as in Crazy Eights.

Other versions include more "power cards" with more specific rules. Scoring is the same as in Crazy Eights.

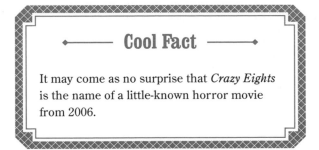

— Cool Fact —

It may come as no surprise that *Crazy Eights* is the name of a little-known horror movie from 2006.

CASINO

Despite its name, Casino is not a gambling game and should not be confused with Poker, Black Jack, and other card games that people play in casinos. Maybe that's why some refer to the game as Cassino, to avoid the confusion. This is a "fishing" game, and it is called such because you're trying to capture cards from a pool in the middle by pairing them with cards in your hand. The origins of the game are uncertain. Some sources say it comes from Italy, while others say it comes from French gambling games of the fifteenth century. Often it is described as a children's game, but the strategy involved can make it fairly challenging—and fun—to play.

RATING: Moderately Challenging

PLAYERS 2–4 players (no partnerships).

DECK One full deck of 52 cards without Jokers.

RANKING Ranking doesn't play a role in this game.

OBJECTIVE To win 21 points. You earn points by capturing as many cards as possible in your turn, by getting the most spades, and by capturing the big point cards.

◇◇

SCORING

Remembering the scoring upfront will help you strategize how to win this game. The primary goal is to collect more cards than any other player, but some cards are worth extra points (see chart on page 32).

◇◇

HOW TO PLAY

DEAL THE CARDS. Dealer gives out four cards per player and places four cards faceup in the middle (players may look at their cards after they have been dealt). After each player runs out of cards in her hand, the dealer gives out four more per player but no new cards are ever dealt to the middle after the first time.

NOTE ⟨ When cards run out in the middle, players are forced to play a card from their hands, thus adding cards back to the middle. (Don't worry; this point will become clear as you play.)

Points for Cards

The player with the most cards at the end of the hand gets 3 points

The player with the most spades at the end of the hand gets 1 point

The player with the 10♦ (Big Casino) gets 2 points

The player with the 2♠ (Little Casino) gets 1 point

Each ace gets 1 point

Each sweep gets 1 point

A sweep is when you pick all of the cards in the middle of the table in one turn. Even if there is just one card in the middle, if you take it, that is a sweep. Remember to keep track of your sweeps as you play.

If you play with two people, you should have a total of six deals (or 48 cards plus the 4 originally dealt to the middle). With three players you have four deals and with four players you have three deals.

PLAYING YOUR TURN. The person to the dealer's left (or opposite the dealer with two players) starts the game. On your turn, you must always play one card. You are trying to capture cards from the four cards laid out in the middle of the table by matching those cards with one in your hand.

The challenging but fun part is that there are *many* ways to capture a card. Here are the possibilities. You may perform only *one* of these options per turn:

Trail a card. You play a single card, laying it faceup alongside the cards dealt faceup in the middle. Usually, this means you have no other play to make (although you may trail a card even if you have other options in your hand). If there are no cards left in the middle, you must trail a card on your turn. Your trailed card is now in play and any player can capture it.

Capture a card by pairing it with a card in your hand. If you have a card in your hand that matches the rank of a card in the middle four, you can take that card.

For example, if you hold the 8♣, and the 8♦ is in the middle, on your turn you show players you have the match and take the 8♦, placing the two cards facedown in front of you.

You can capture more than one card a turn this way. If the center holds the 8♦, 8♠, and 8♥, you can use your 8♣ to take all three cards.

NOTE   **The face cards are the exception to this rule.** You can pair face cards (K, Q, J), but you can capture only single pairs. In other words, if the Q♣, Q♥, and Q♦ are on the table, you can capture only one of them with the Q♠ in your hand.

Capture cards in combination. You can also take cards that add up to the sum of a single card in your hand. For example, if you hold the 10♣, you can pick up:

6♦ and 4♠ or 9♥ and ace ♠ (aces count as one).

Or if the cards in the center are 3♥, 2♦, A♦, and 4♣, you can use your 10♣ to sweep the table and pick up all those cards because added together they equal 10.

NOTE You are always using *one* card from your hand to pick up cards on the table. For example, you cannot use a 4♠ and a 3♥ in your hand to pick up a 7♦ on the table.

But that's not all! A card can take sets of cards that equal the sum of its face value. For example, if you hold a 10♣ you can pick up the following cards from the middle:

4♦, 6♠ [together = 10] and 3♥, 7♥ [together = 10]

You can take both of these sets in one turn (again—another sweep!).

Build combinations. You can use the cards in your hand to build on one of the cards in the middle in order to capture it. There are two ways to build:

VALUE BUILD. You add the value of one card from your hand to another card in the center, so that the sum of this build equals the value of another card in your hand. For example: One of the center cards is a 3♥.

You have a 6♦ and 9♠ in your hand.

On your turn, you can lay your 6♦ on top of the 3♥ and declare that you are "building 9s." On your next turn, you can pick up the 6♦ and 3♥ with your 9♠. However, any other player with a 9 can pick up the combination you made as well.

PAIRING BUILD. You can also make builds by pairing cards of the same rank. For example: One of the center cards is a 6♦.

You have a 6♣ and 6♠ in your hand.

On your turn, you can lay your 6♣ on top of the 6♦ and say "building 6s." On your next turn you can show your 6♠ and pick up all the 6s.

After making the build, you can do any of the following on your next turn:

Pick up your build (as described above).

Capture a different card from the center and leave your build on the table.

Increase your build. For example, suppose you have a build of 9 on the table (made up of a 6♦ and 3♥). You have a 10♥ and an ace♦ in your hand.

On your turn, you could add an ace♦ to the 6♦ and 3♥ and say you're increasing the build and are now building 10s.

On the next turn you use your 10♥ to pick up the ace♦, 6♦, and 3♥.

Pair your build. You can pair your build with a card from your hand that matches the total value of your build on the table. Again, suppose you have a build of the 6♦ and 3♥ on the table.

You have both a 9♣ and a 9♠ in your hand.

On your turn, you can pair the 9♣ with the 6♦ and 3♥. Once you have paired your build, no one can increase the build. The value is locked.

On your next turn, you can pick up the 9♣, 6♦, and 3♥ with your 9♠.

ENDING THE HAND. The hand ends when none of the players are holding cards. If all cards have been played and there are still cards in the middle that have gone unclaimed, then the player who last captured a card gets those remaining cards. This does not count as a sweep.

- **You cannot start a build using two cards in the center of the table.** You must start a build by playing a card from your hand. So, if there are two 10s faceup in the middle, you cannot put the two 10s together and say "building 10s."

- **Similarly, you cannot increase a build using a card in the center of the table.** So, if the center cards include a build of a 6♦ and 3♥ next to an ace♦, you cannot move the ace♦ on top of this build and say "building 10s."

- **However, you can pair a build by using a card in the center of the table.** So, if the center card includes a build of a 6♦ and 3♥ next to a 9♦, you can move the 9♦ on top of this build and say "building 9s." This is the only occasion when you can move a card on the table to another card on the table.

- **You can capture and increase any build on the table** (not just your own).

- **You cannot "fake" a build.** In other words, you can't combine a 6♦ and 3♥ and declare that you are "building 9s" unless you have a 9 in your hand. This same rule applies to increasing a build.

STRATEGY

Casino gets more interesting as you internalize the rules and recognize opportunities for picking up as many cards as possible during your turn.

EXAMPLE ◄ Suppose the following cards are on the center of the table:

You have the 5♣ and 9♠ in your hand.

In one turn, you can pair your 5♣ with the 4♦, making a new build of 9s.

On your next turn, you have the potential to pick up the build of 3♠, 6♦, 9♣, and the build of 5♣ and 4♦ with your 9♠.

◇◇

SCORING

When all the cards have been played, the players count the points from the cards they have won based on the scoring system on page 32.

After points have been tallied, the player to the dealer's left becomes the dealer.

Keep playing hands until one player scores 21 points and wins.

II

To a non–card player, *taking a trick* sounds like an activity performed at a magic show. It's actually the principal concept behind many popular card games. Start with Whist and graduate to Hearts as soon as you need a little more of a challenge. Try Euchre when you are ready to experience quirky card rankings and the process of "ordering up" the trump (a precursor to the bidding process in Chapter IV games).

WHIST (AND SCOTCH WHIST), 4 PLAYERS

HEARTS, 3–5 PLAYERS

EUCHRE (AND HASENPFEFFER), 4 PLAYERS

WHIST

Whist, like the game Euchre, is a great introduction to a few fundamentals that are the basis for Bridge. It is simple and easy to learn. Whist originated in Britain and was widely popular in the eighteenth and nineteenth centuries. Some say the name is derived from *wistful*, which can mean pensive or attentive. Benjamin Franklin, Henry Clay, Nathaniel Hawthorne, Napoleon, and Washington Irving played the game, and Edgar Allan Poe was such a fan that he featured it in his story "Murders in the Rue Morgue." The characters in Jane Austen's *Pride and Prejudice* while away the hours playing whist.

RATING Easy

PLAYERS 4 players. In this traditional version of Whist, there are two teams of two. Partners sit across from each other, and each partnership scores, rather than each player.

DECK One full deck of 52 cards without Jokers.

RANKING Standard ranking with ace high and 2 low.

OBJECTIVE The first team to score 7 points wins.

◇◇

HOW TO PLAY

DEAL THE CARDS. Dealer passes out all the cards, facedown, 13 to each player, one at a time—except the final card, which the dealer places faceup. The suit of this card will be trump for the hand. Trump suit cards beat all other suits (regardless of the rank of the card). Once all players have seen this card, the dealer returns it to her hand.

TAKING TRICKS. To get points, teams must win tricks. Tricks are simply a round of cards that each player places in the middle. To begin, the player to the dealer's left (the eldest) puts any card from her hand in the center of the table, establishing the leading suit for that trick.

Going clockwise around the table, each player then has to follow suit. The player who puts down the highest card in that suit wins the pile, unless someone plays a card in the trump suit.

If a player cannot follow suit, she may play a trump suit card or any other suit. A trump card of any rank will win the trick; any other suit will not win. If two players put down a trump card, the higher trump card wins.

EXAMPLE ◄ Dealer shows a 3♦ as the final card dealt, making diamond the trump suit.

Eldest   **Player 2**   **Player 3**   **Dealer**

A♣   8♣   4♣   5♦

The eldest (first to the dealer's left) starts the game with the high A♣, thinking that everyone probably has at least one club and will have to follow suit.

PLAYER 2 has clubs, so she plays the 8♣.

PLAYER 3, the partner of the eldest, also has clubs and plays the lowest in her hand (4♣)—saving higher clubs for a possible win later in the hand.

THE DEALER, however, has no clubs. So she plays her lowest trump card (5♦) and wins the trick. She collects the cards in the center and places the pile by her side.

Remember, as you play, you're not just trying to win tricks for yourself. You're working with a partner, so you have to be sensitive and aware of the cards that your partner is playing.

After each trick, the trick winner begins the next round, placing a card in the center.

ENDING THE HAND. At the end of the hand, after all 13 cards are played, teams tally their tricks. Then the next player to the left becomes dealer and a new round begins.

SCORING

You might expect that you should win one point for each trick but scoring doesn't work that way. A team must win more than 6 tricks to get a point. If a team wins 7 tricks, for example, it gets 1 point. If a team only wins 5 tricks, it doesn't get any points.

VARIATION

SCOTCH WHIST

You can call this Whist with a Twist. Scotch Whist is a variation on Whist that is also known as Catch the Ten (possibly because winning the trump 10 offers some big points) and Catch Honors. If you want to really get in the mood, you might want to play it with a glass of scotch in hand. You may need a scotch to wrap your head around the rules.

DECK 36 cards, ace through 6.

RANKING Traditional ranking with ace high and 6 low, except in the trump suit, jack is high.

So, if ♥ is the trump suit, then the ranking is J♥, A♥, K♥, Q♥, 10♥, 9♥, 8♥, 7♥, 6♥. Cards in all other suits follow the standard rank.

OBJECTIVE First team to score 41 points wins.

HOW TO PLAY

DEAL THE CARDS. Dealer passes out all the cards facedown, nine to each player, one at a time—except the final card, which the dealer places faceup. The suit of the face-up card will be trump for the hand. Once all players have seen the card, the dealer returns it to his hand.

TAKING TRICKS. Play is exactly the same as regular Whist, however, since trump cards won in tricks provide valuable points, your strategy is based on trying to win these cards.

SCORING

These trump cards provide the following points when won in tricks:

JACK = 11 points
10 = 10 points
ACE = 4 points
KING = 3 points
QUEEN = 2 points

First, both partnerships tally up the number of points earned by the trump cards in their piles.

Next, if your partnership wins the majority of tricks (5 or more) you get additional points. To calculate these points, take the total number of cards that you've won and subtract 18 (the number of cards you and your partner were originally dealt). So if your partnership won 6 tricks:

6 tricks x 4 cards = 24 cards – 18 cards = 6 additional points

The first team to get 41 points wins. If there is a tie, you can play another hand and see who then has the most points.

HEARTS

The origin of Hearts goes back to a game from mid-eighteenth-century Spain called Reversis, where you're penalized for winning tricks. In many ways, there's a perverse logic to Hearts because you *don't* want to win the tricks with hearts in them. People call it a cutthroat game because you're often throwing out cards that will hurt your friends. Hearts became popular in the United States in the 1880s, but some say it was played as far back colonial times. In the 1920s, the queen of spades was added into the game as a card you absolutely don't want to win. Nicknamed the "Black Mariah," this card can cost you big points. Other unique rules have been introduced along the way, but the following rules represent one of the most common versions of the game.

RATING Medium

PLAYERS Best played with 3–5 players.

DECK One full deck of 52 cards without Jokers.

RANKING Ace high to 2 low.

OBJECTIVE To score as few points as possible. You play to 100 points, and whoever goes over 100 first loses. Then, whoever has the fewest points wins.

SCORING You want to avoid winning the cards that score points.

Points for Cards

EVERY HEART WON IN A TRICK = 1 point
THE QUEEN OF SPADES =13 points

HOW TO PLAY

DEAL THE CARDS. Dealer gives one card to each player, clockwise, until the entire deck is dealt. If there are three players, the extra card is placed aside facedown. It is called the kitty, and it is counted into the first trick-winner's score at the end of the hand. With five players, two cards end up in the kitty.

PLAYING YOUR TURN. This is a trick-taking game, except you *don't* want to win tricks with hearts in them, and you absolutely want to avoid winning the dreaded queen of spades (the "Black Mariah"). Play proceeds as follows:

Arrange your hand. Group suits together and organize them by rank.

Pass three cards. Before play begins, players follow a unique rule of passing three cards of their choosing to another player.

ON the first hand, you pass three cards to the player on your left.
ON the second hand, you pass three cards to the player on your right.
ON the third hand, you pass three cards to the player opposite you.
ON the fourth hand, you don't pass cards.

These passing rules repeat after the fourth hand. With three and five players, you skip the third-hand pass because there's no one opposite you.

How do you decide which cards to pass?

- You might want to pass the king and ace of spades because if you play those, and someone with the queen of spades has to follow suit, then you will win the deadly Black Mariah.

- Pass other high suit cards—aces, kings, etc.—because they may increase your likelihood of winning a trick with a heart in it.

- If you are dealt the Black Mariah, you might decide to pass it to another player (but remember who you passed it to!)

- Low cards are best to keep because they often lose tricks. Keep as many low spades as you can; they will help you avoid winning the Black Mariah.

TAKING TRICKS. Once you have traded your three cards, play begins for real and works like all other trick-taking games, but there is no trump. The first card played is always the 2♣. Whoever has that card places it in the middle and begins the trick. Each player to that person's left must follow suit if he can. If you can't follow suit, you may play any other card in your hand. A few rules:

- If you have no clubs to play in the first trick, you *cannot* play a heart or the queen of spades.

- After the first trick, a heart can be played by a non-leading player who is not able to follow suit. This is called "breaking" the suit. Once the suit is broken, anyone can start playing hearts.

The player who tosses out the highest card of the leading suit wins the trick. Remember that if you can't follow suit, you can't win the trick (this can be a good thing, especially when players start tossing out hearts).

Whoever wins the trick starts off the next one by putting a card in the middle, which determines the suit for that trick. Remember that if you lead a trick with a suit that none of the other players can follow, you automatically win this trick (this is a bad thing when the other players start tossing out hearts).

If you're playing with three or five players and you realize the 2♣ is in the kitty, you can just start play to the dealer's left.

EXAMPLE You are dealt: 8♥, 3♥, Q♠,7♠, 5♠, 2♠, J♦, 9♦, 3♦, K♣, Q♣, 9♣, 7♣

You have to decide which cards to pass. Since you don't want the Q♠, you might pass that, and you have a lot of high clubs, so you might pass the K♣ and Q♣ as well. There is no surefire winning strategy, but you will know who has the Q♠ and you'll try not to win it back.

Another player passes the K♠, 8♣, and 10♣ to you. The K♠ is especially dangerous because if you have to follow suit in spades and that's all you have left, you will be at risk of winning back the Q♠. Fortunately, you have the 7♠, 5♠, and 2♠ to play before you are forced to toss out the K♠.

EXAMPLE Here are the first three tricks and how the players play the cards:

1ST TRICK

PLAYER 1 leads with the 2♣

PLAYER 2 puts down the 6♣

YOU are **PLAYER 3**. Since winning this hand is harmless, you play your 9♣.

PLAYER 4 also decides to discard a high card and puts out the A♣, winning that trick.

2ND TRICK

PLAYER 4 (the winner) leads with the K♣

PLAYER 1 puts down the 5♣

PLAYER 2 breaks the hearts suit with the Q♥

It's your turn to play a card. You have to play clubs to follow suit and you will be safe playing your 10♣ this time. But you make a mental note that the player to your right played the Q♥, meaning he has no more clubs to play. Player 4 unluckily takes the trick with his K♣ and scores one point because he wins the Q♥ in that trick.

3RD TRICK

PLAYER 4 (the winner) leads again with the 8♦

PLAYER 1 puts down the 10♦

PLAYER 2 puts down the 7♦

You decide to play the J♦ and win the trick. In this case, winning is harmless, because none of these cards score points.

ENDING THE HAND. When all cards have been played, the hand is over and points are tallied. Then the next player to the left deals.

STRATEGY

- **When you pass cards, remember what you're passing.** That can influence your play. Note when someone can't follow suit. That will help you determine what future cards to play. Keep your low cards, get rid of your high cards—that decreases the danger of winning hearts or the queen of spades.

- **Eliminate a suit in your hand.** When you're void of a suit, you don't have to follow the lead and you can't win the trick. This can open up a door for you to discard high-ranking cards or—better yet—your hearts (which will give unwanted points to your opponent).

- **One advanced move is called "shooting the moon."** In rare cases, you may be able to win all the hearts and the queen of spades; if you succeed, each of your opponents gets 26 points. As a beginner, you shouldn't concern yourself with this rule, but as you play more you may occasionally see an opportunity to shoot the moon.

◇◇

SCORING

Add up the points for the cards that you have won (each heart is worth 1 point and the Black Mariah is worth 13 points). Once any player's score goes over 100, the game ends. Highest score loses and lowest score wins.

Cool Fact

"Hearts in Atlantis" is a short story by Stephen King revolving around a dorm full of college students addicted to playing Hearts. King also mentions the game in his novel *Skeleton Crew.* Once you start playing, you'll see how the game is incredibly addicting.

EUCHRE

Euchre is said to have originated in the Alsace region of France near the border of Germany from a game called *Juckerspiel*. Euchre is a morphing of the word *Jucker,* which refers to the jack. In this game, the jack in the trump suit is the most powerful card. Euchre's claim to fame is that it introduced the Joker to the deck. In the 1860s, the British created a new card for the game, known as the Imperial Bower or Best Bower. It is basically a super jack that can trump all other cards, including the trump jack. In time, this card transformed into today's Joker. In the standard U.S. version of Euchre, however, the Joker is not used. Euchre is popular is western New York and the Midwest, especially in Michigan and Ohio, where some say German settlers introduced it in the nineteenth century.

RATING Medium

PLAYERS 4 Players. In this version, there are two teams of two. Partners sit across from each other, and each partnership scores, rather than each player.

DECK 24-card Euchre is most common in the United States, using the 9, 10, J, Q, K, and A.

RANKING From highest to lowest, jack of the trump (also called right bower), jack of the suit with the color of trump (also called left bower), A, K, Q, J, 10, 9. (Note that non-trump jacks have their usual ranking.)

If hearts are trump, then the ranking is J♥, J♦, A♥, K♥, Q♥, 10♥, 9♥.

In this example, J♥ is the right bower and J♦ is the left bower. A quirky rule of Euchre is that J♦ is no longer considered part of the diamond suit. In effect, it leaves its suit and becomes a heart and the second most powerful card in the trump suit.

OBJECTIVE First team to score 10 points wins.

◇◇

HOW TO PLAY

DEAL THE CARDS. Because this game is all about the jacks, a common way to choose the dealer is to distribute a card to each player until one gets a jack—then that person deals. Each player gets five cards; a common way is to deal two to the player at the left, then three to the next person, then two to the next, and three to the dealer. In the next round, the dealer gives out three, two, three, and two, so each player has five cards. The remaining four cards are placed in the middle of the table. The dealer flips over the top card and places this card on top of the other three.

Determining the trump. Players decide which suit will be trump for each hand based on the face-up card in the middle of the table. If this card is selected as trump, it will be the dominant boss suit for the round—more powerful than all the others.

To start the process, the player to the dealer's left (called the eldest hand) consults the cards in his hand and decides whether he wants to accept or reject the turned-up card for trump. If he wants that card's suit to be trump, he says, "I order it up." If he rejects it, he says, "Pass."

If the eldest hand passes, then the dealer's partner goes through the same process. He can either accept the card by saying "I assist," or pass. If he passes, the third player can then either accept by saying "I order it up," or pass. If all three players have passed, then the dealer has a turn to accept or pass.

EXAMPLE ⟨ Suppose the turned-up card is the 9♥.

You are the eldest hand and holding J♥, J♦, A♥, K♥, and Q♥. Since you hold high-ranking hearts and the J♦ (left bower), you will definitely want to "order it up" because every card you have will win a trick.

After a player orders up the trump, the dealer takes the card and exchanges it for any other card in his hand. The card the dealer has exchanged for the trump card is placed facedown on the remaining three cards in the middle of the table, and those four cards are put out of play for the hand. (In rare cases, the dealer may return the turn-up card if he doesn't want it—but usually the dealer keeps it because it is a trump card.)

If all players reject the trump in the first go-around, then the card is placed faceup partially underneath the pack. Then the eldest hand has the option of simply naming the trump suit for that hand or passing. In the rare case that all four players pass in round two, then all cards are returned to the deck and the next player becomes the dealer, starting the process over again.

TAKING TRICKS. Once trump is declared, the real play begins. Each player has five cards, so there are five possible tricks (or "rounds" of play).

The eldest (player to dealer's left) goes first, determining the suit for this trick by placing a card in the center. Each player to the left then must follow suit. If you can't follow suit, you can play either a trump suit card or any other card in your hand. To win the trick, you need to play either the highest of the suit or a card in the trump suit. If there's more than one trump card in the trick, the highest trump card wins. Again, if you can't follow suit or play a trump suit card, you will have to put in a card that has no chance of winning.

EXAMPLE   Trump is ♣.

1ST TRICK

Eldest Hand	Dealer's Partner	Eldest's Partner	Dealer
A♠	10♠	J♦	Q♠

Eldest wins and picks up the cards and wins that trick.

2ND TRICK

Eldest Hand	Dealer's Partner	Eldest's Partner	Dealer
A♣	J♠	9♥	10♦

Dealer's partner picks up the trick (all four cards). J♠ is the left bower so although A♣ is strong, J♠ beats it.

Remember that you are trying to win tricks for you and your partner, so play your cards with your partner in mind as well.

The winner of the trick picks up the four cards and keeps them in a separate pile. Then he leads the next trick.

ENDING THE HAND. When you've played all five of your cards, that hand is over. Add up the number of hands that your team has won and tally scores according to the rules below. The next person to the dealer's left becomes the dealer for the next hand. Continue to play hands until one team scores 10 points to win.

◇◇

STRATEGY

INTO THE VOID. You will figure out the subtleties and strategies as you play, but you may want to look for opportunities to get rid of a card in your hand early on that is not trump if that will "create a void." A void means you no longer have that suit in your hand, so you may not have to follow suit as your hand progresses, and that could help you win if you're holding trump cards.

EXAMPLE You are left of the dealer, and you are dealt the following hand.

You: J♠, J♣, 9♥, A♦, K♠

The turn-up card in the middle is 9♠. You have the first turn to declare whether ♠ is the trump suit for this hand.

You want to "order it up." You are holding the right bower (J♠), the most powerful card in the game. You also possess the left bower (J♣), which has left its suit and become a spade. It is now the second most powerful card in the game. You also have K♠, which is a strong trump card. You have two sure-winning tricks in your hand, and you have to hope to win another. You know the dealer has the trump 9♠, but you can easily beat that if you play your jacks right.

Possible strategy: You might start with the 9♥ first to create a void and get rid of a low, sure-to-lose card early. Besides, your partner may still win. From there, you have to see how the game flows, but odds are in your favor that you and your partner can win.

◇◇

SCORING

If you are the maker (the one who declares trump), you have to win three or four tricks to get 1 point or five tricks to get 2 points. Five tricks is called a march. If you declare the trump in the beginning of the round, and you fail to get three tricks, you are "euchred" and the opposing partnership wins two points.

Penalties. If you fail to follow suit when you can, that's called a renege. You're supposed to correct this type of mistake before the winner picks up the trick. But if the opposing teams catches your mistake, they can either take an additional two points or subtract two from you.

In the Barn. In many variations of Euchre, you have to announce when you're a point away from winning. A typical practice when you hit 9 points is to say, loudly, "We are in the barn."

Going It Alone. If the caller of trump has an exceptionally good hand and thinks he can win all five tricks on his own, he has the option to go it alone and potentially win more points. If you say you're going it alone, your partner puts his hand facedown and out of play, and this hand becomes a three-way game. If you win all five tricks going it alone, you get 4 points. If you get three or four tricks, you still score the usual 1 point. If you get euchred, your opposing team gets the usual two points.

VARIATION

HASENPFEFFER

Hasenpfeffer, or peppered hare, is a German rabbit stew. It is also a name for a variation of Euchre that involves bidding. Bidding means you are predicting how many tricks you will win in a hand. In a sense, you are bidding in regular Euchre when you declare trump because you are predicting that you will make at least three tricks. Hasenpfeffer requires that you make a precise bid or prediction of how many tricks you expect to win.

NOTE ◄ If bidding is a totally unfamiliar concept to you, try some of the easy bidding games in chapter four before attempting this one.

DECK Hasenpfeffer uses the same cards as regular Euchre but has the bonus of adding in the Joker, which will trump all other cards.

HOW TO PLAY

The dealer distributes six cards to each player, one at a time. The last is placed facedown on the table. The eldest hand starts a round of bidding. Each player can bid once from 1 to 6—predicting the number of tricks she and her partner will win, or the player can pass (not make a bid). You are not consulting with your partner on what to bid, but you are guessing how many tricks you might win working together with your partner. If no one bids, the person holding the Joker has to make a bid of 3.

The highest bid declares trump. That person takes the card in the middle and discards one that will be out of play. Partnerships win 1 point for each trick won. However, if a team can't make its bid, the team loses the amount of the bid. Teams play to 10 points.

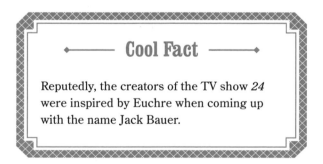

Cool Fact

Reputedly, the creators of the TV show *24* were inspired by Euchre when coming up with the name Jack Bauer.

III

Melding games are often a fun way to play collaboratively with a partner. *Melding* is combining the cards in your hand into groups of three or more cards, then laying them on the table to score points. As you move from Rummy and Gin Rummy to Canasta, the scoring systems and the rules for forming melds grow more complicated. Start with a few simple games of Rummy if you are totally new to this family of games.

RUMMY (AND 500 RUMMY), 2–4 PLAYERS

GIN RUMMY, 2–6 PLAYERS

HAND AND FOOT, 4 PLAYERS

CANASTA, 4 PLAYERS

RUMMY

Rummy games began in the early 1900s and are thought to have originated from a Mexican card game called Conquian or from a card game in Romania. There are a few theories on where Rummy gets its name. "Rum" is British slang meaning odd or peculiar, and Brits may have thought this game to be strange when it was first introduced. Others say that losers of the game would buy a round of rum for the players. Another idea is that it comes from "rumbullion" or "rumbustion," meaning great tumult or uproar. Basic Rummy is easy to learn and the level of challenge can be fairly low, but it is the foundation for many other more clever games like Rummy 500, Gin Rummy, and Canasta.

RATING Easy

PLAYERS 2–4 players (can be played with 6).

DECK One full deck of 52 cards without Jokers.

RANKING Standard ranking, but with ace low to king high.

OBJECTIVE To be the first to get rid of all the cards in your hand.

SCORING The cards left in your hand add points to the winner's score.

◆—— Points for Cards ——◆

K, Q, J = 10 points each
ACE = 1 point each
NUMBER CARDS = Their face value (for example, 6♥ =
6 points and 8♣ = 8 points)

HOW TO PLAY

DEAL THE CARDS. Distribute one card to each player, clockwise.
Here's how to deal the cards, depending on the number of players:

2 PLAYERS: Each gets 10 cards.
3–6 PLAYERS: Each gets 6 cards.

Once all players have cards, put the remainder of the deck (the stock)
in the middle, and flip the top card over faceup by its side to start the
discard pile.

Arrange your hand. Look at your cards and arrange them in terms of melds.

Melds are combinations of three or more cards. There are two types of melds:

SEQUENCES *(or runs).* Three or more cards of the same suit in numerical order. For example: 6♠, 7♠, 8♠ or 10♥, J♥, Q♥, and K♥

GROUPS *(or sets, or books).* Three or more cards of the same face value or rank. For example: A♦, A♣, A♥ or 9♠, 9♣, 9♥, 9♦

PLAYING YOUR TURN. The player to the dealer's left (the eldest) goes first. On your turn, take one card either from the top of the stock or the discard pile, and then play as follows:

Meld your cards. If you are holding a meld, consider whether you want to lay it down on the table in front of you. Melding is optional and you can only lay down one meld per turn. So if you have A♦, 2♦, and 3♦ in your hand and 7♠, 7♣, and 7♥, you can lay only *one* of those combinations down on your turn if you choose to.

Lay off. Laying off means adding cards in your hand to existing melds on the table. You can add cards to melds that have been set down by you *or* your opponents. Laying off is also optional.

Discard a card. After you are done melding and/or laying off, then you must discard one card from your hand and place it faceup on the discard pile.

NOTE If you drew from the discard pile at the start of your turn, you cannot discard the same card on that turn. The discard pile must have a new card on top with each turn. If you took a card from the stock at the beginning of your turn, you can discard that card if you wish.

If cards run out in the stock and the player whose turn it is does not want the card in the discard pile, the discard pile is shuffled and turned over. That becomes the stock and play continues.

ENDING THE HAND. The hand ends when one player gets rid of all the cards in his hand by either melding, laying off, or discarding. This is called going out. A player does not have to discard to go out. At that point, no other player may meld, lay off, or discard.

A player is said to go "rummy" if he can meld his entire hand in one turn.

NOTE Sometimes, toward the end, the play can get "stuck." Players are holding cards that others want and the game will not end unless those cards are played. Once the discard pile becomes the stock, set the limit that players can only go through the discard pile two more times before ending the hand.

At the end of each hand, the new deal goes to the winner.

SCORING

The player who goes out first wins the hand. When one player goes out, the other players add up the points in their hands.

EXAMPLE You go out (winning the hand); one of your opponents is holding cards worth 21 points and the other opponent is holding cards worth 7 points. Your score for this hand is 28 points.

In the rare case that no one goes out, each player tallies the points in his hand and then the player with the least points wins and gets the points from the other players.

EXAMPLE You're holding 8 points, one opponent is holding 10 points, and the other opponent is holding 13 points. You are the winner and score 23 points.

The game is played until one player scores an agreed upon number of points (100, 200, 300, etc.) Alternatively, you can play up to an agreed upon number of hands (whoever has the highest score after five hands wins the game).

OPTIONAL RULES

These are common rules that can be added into versions of the game you play. You should discuss these alternatives with the other players and agree on which rules to play by.

Multiple meld rule. You are allowed to lay down more than one meld in a turn.

Bonus for going out before making any meld or laying off. You get a bonus for going out before laying any cards on the table. Some call this "going rummy." A bonus may be doubling the points earned or getting an extra 10 points.

No laying off until you have melded. You cannot lay off any cards until you have melded.

Ace can be high or low. The value of the ace can be played as either high or low.

Going out by discard only. You may only go out by discarding your final card—not melding or laying off.

Block Rummy. The discard pile is never used again as the stock.

VARIATION

◆
500 RUMMY OR RUMMY 500
◆

This is a pumped-up version of Rummy that increases the strategy and game play. It also goes by 500 Rum or sometimes Pinochle Rummy. There are many different types of play in this version of rummy, which makes it more challenging and interesting than straight-up rummy.

PLAYERS 2 or more players

DECK One full deck of 52 cards without Jokers for 2 to 4 players; two full decks of cards for 5 players or more.

RANKING Standard ranking, but ace can be played either high or low.

OBJECTIVE To be the first to get rid of all your cards and to score points.

SCORING In Rummy 500, there are additional point values assigned to sequences of cards left in your hand.

∞∞

HOW TO PLAY

DEAL THE CARDS. Distribute one card to each player, clockwise. Here's how to distribute the cards, depending on the number of players:

2 PLAYERS: 13 cards each
3 OR MORE PLAYERS: 7 cards each

Put the remainder of the deck (the stock) in the middle, and flip the top card over faceup by its side to begin the discard pile.

← —— Points for Cards —— →

K, Q, J = 10 points each
ACES score as follows:

- **IN LOW SEQUENCES (A, 2, 3), ACE** = 1 point

- **IN HIGH SEQUENCES (Q, K, A), ACE** = 15 points

- **IN GROUPS (A ♥, A♣, A♦), EACH ACE** = 15 points

- **UNMELDED ACES** = 15 points

NUMBER CARDS = Their face value (6♥ = 6 points and an 8♣ = 8 points)

Arrange your hand. As with regular Rummy, you want to arrange your cards in terms of melds (see page 62).

PLAYING YOUR HAND. The player to the dealer's left goes first. On your turn, choose one of the two options for drawing a card:

Take the top card from the stock or the top card from the discard pile. If you take a card from either the top of the stock or the top of the discard pile, you can keep it in your hand, use it with other cards in your hand to lay down in a meld, or add it to any existing melds on the table.

Take a card from deeper in the discard pile. In Rummy 500, you also have the option of taking a card that is deeper in the discard pile. The discard pile is built by fanning out or overlapping the cards faceup as they are discarded, so you can always see each card. There are a few rules for drawing deeper from the discard pile:

- The card that you select from within the discard pile must be used during your turn to create a new meld or be added to an existing meld.

- You must also take all the cards *above* your selected card. Using the rest of these cards during your turn is optional. They can either stay in your hand or be used for melding.

Melding. In Rummy 500, you can lay down as many melds as you want in one turn. So if you have A♦, 2♦, and 3♦ in your hand and 7♠, 7♣, and 7♥, you could lay down both of those combinations on your turn if you choose to. Melding is optional.

Laying off. You can also add cards to your melds or to any player's melds on the table. The cards that you "lay off" on another player's melds will also be counted as points that are added to your score at the end of a hand. When you lay off to another player's meld, you set the card on the table with your own cards and tell the other players exactly how you're playing that card.

EXAMPLE Your opponent has a meld with a J♠, Q♠, and K♠ on the table in front of him.

In your hand is a 10♠, which means that you can add to your opponent's meld. You place the 10♠ in front of you and tell your opponents which meld will include your 10♠. No one else can add the 10♠ to that meld (a possibility if you are playing with two decks).

Discard a card. After you have done all of your melding and laying off, your turn is over and you must discard one card from your hand and place it faceup on the discard pile.

ENDING THE HAND. The hand ends when one player has no cards left. That player may discard a final card or meld all his cards. Alternatively, the play ends when the stock is gone and one player cannot or will not draw from the discard pile. At the end of each hand, the new deal goes to the winner.

◇◇

STRATEGY

There is a lot of strategy in Rummy when it comes to picking up the discard cards. If you pick up a lot of cards, you can potentially create or add to melds and score a lot of points. You may also wind up stuck with cards in your hand if someone goes out.

As the game progresses, you typically want to get high cards and melds out of your hand so you will not have as many points to subtract if the game should end before you go out.

◇◇

SCORING

When one player goes out, all of the players add up the card points in their melds on the table. Players who are still holding cards must subtract the points value for all of the cards left in their hands.

Even melded cards are subtracted from your score if they are still in your hand when another player goes out (so in this game, you may want to get your melds on the table quickly).

There are no bonus points for going out first.

The game is played to 500 points.

GIN RUMMY

Many game experts say that Gin Rummy was created at the beginning of the 1900s by Elwood Baker, a member of the Knickerbocker Whist Club. Because Rummy brought to mind the alcohol, Baker named this game after another type of booze—gin. Often just called Gin, the game became very popular, especially in the late 1920s and the 1940s. The plot of the Pulitzer Prize–winning play *The Gin Game* revolves around an elderly couple playing the game. Shirley MacLaine and Jack Lemmon form a bond over Gin Rummy in the movie *The Apartment*. The humorist Dave Barry wrote: "Rummy offers a fine line between mental illness and hobby."

RATING Medium

PLAYERS 2–6 Players (most commonly played with 2).

DECK One full deck of 52 cards without Jokers.

RANKING Standard ranking, but with ace low to king high.

OBJECTIVE To make melds in your hand and win points by achieving the lowest number of points in unmelded cards at the end of the hand. The game is played to 100 points.

SCORING Points are the same value as for Rummy.

Points for Cards

K, Q, J = 10 points each
ACES = 1 point each
NUMBER CARDS = Their face value

HOW TO PLAY

DEAL THE CARDS. Distribute one card at a time to each player, clockwise. Here's how to distribute the cards, depending on the number of players:

2 PLAYERS: 10 cards each
3–4 PLAYERS: 7 cards each
5–6 PLAYERS: 6 cards each

Once all players have cards, put the remainder of the deck (called the stock) in the middle, and flip the top card over by its side to begin the discard pile.

Arrange your hand. Like Rummy, you want to arrange your cards in terms of possible melds (see page 62).

PLAYING YOUR TURN. The player to the dealer's left goes first. On your turn, you play as follows:

Melding your cards. Take one card from the top of the stock or the discard pile. Use this card to add to the melds in your hand (as you would in regular Rummy); however, in this version, you DO NOT lay down melds on the table as you play. Keep them in your hand.

Discard a card. Discard one card to conclude your turn.

Knock to end the hand (if you think you are winning). When you think the total value of your *unmelded* cards (deadwood) is lower than any of the other players', you knock on the table, signaling to the other players that you are ending the hand. At this stage, all players show their hands, laying all melds and unmelded cards on the table. Knocking has a few rules:

- You can knock only after you've drawn a card and put a discard card facedown on the discard pile.

- You must have deadwood of 10 points or less to knock.

- If you knock, your opponent(s) can lay off cards on your melds before the scoring takes place.

- If you knock and have no deadwood, that's called "going Gin." You win the hand and your opponent(s) cannot lay off cards on your meld. If you go Gin, you get the score from the opponent's deadwood plus 25 points.

ENDING THE HAND. Once a player has knocked, and the other opponents are finished laying off their cards on the knocker's melds, everyone tallies their deadwood points to determine who won the round.

At the end of each hand, the new deal goes to the winner.

◇◇◇

SCORING

After one player knocks and his opponents have finished laying off cards on his melds, ALL of the players tally the value of their unmelded cards (deadwood) ONLY.

The winner of the hand has the lowest deadwood score, but the winner's FINAL score for the hand is determined as follows:

You knock and your deadwood scores lowest. If your deadwood score is 6 and the other two players' deadwood scores are 8 and 10, your final score is 12 (the sum of your opponents deadwood, minus your own).

You knock and go Gin. You have no deadwood and the other two players' deadwood scores are 8 and 10. You simply take the sum of your opponents' deadwood scores (18) and add a 25-point bonus. Your final score is 43 points.

You knock, but another player ends up with an equal or lower deadwood score. If your deadwood score is 8 and the other two players' deadwood scores are 8 and 10, the player who is tied with you gets 10 deadwood points (the sum of all of his opponents' deadwood, minus his own), plus a 25-point bonus (35 points total). You do not score any points.

You knock, but more than one player ends up with lower deadwood scores. If your deadwood score is 8 and the other two players' scores are 6 and 4, the player with the lowest deadwood score gets 10 deadwood points (the sum of all her opponents' deadwood, minus her own), plus a 10-point bonus (20 points total).

Play usually goes to 100 points.

VARIATIONS

KNOCK RUMMY

The same rules of Gin Rummy apply, with the following minor differences:

- You don't need a minimum of 10 deadwood points or less to knock; you can knock whenever you think you're holding the lowest-scoring deadwood.

- When you knock, your opponents do not lay off their cards on your melds before scoring.

OKLAHOMA GIN

A very popular version where the amount for knocking is set by the turn-up card after the deal. If the turn up card is a 4♠, you must have deadwood of 4 or less to knock.

HAND AND FOOT

Hand and Foot is a popular game throughout North America, and it has *many* variations. It features the elements of Canasta, and in all versions players have two stacks of cards—one called the hand and one called the foot. Part of the fun is the huge number of cards required to play, as well as tossing around the amusing terms used to describe groups of cards: *clean piles*, *dirty piles*, and *wild piles*.

RATING Medium

PLAYERS The game can be played with 2 to 6 players but the best version (described here) is with 4 people playing in two partnerships.

DECK This game requires FIVE full decks with two Jokers per deck for a total of 270 cards.

RANKING Hand and Foot is all about building melds and scoring points (see the scoring section to learn the point values for each card). Ranking doesn't come into the play of the game.

OBJECTIVE The team who has the most points after four hands wins.

SCORING Knowing the value of the cards and how they score points is an important aspect of this game. Ideally, all players should keep a copy of the score chart (see pages 76–77) in front of them. Beginners should also keep the rules for melds and piles handy.

◇◇

HOW TO PLAY

DEAL THE CARDS. Shuffle all five decks together. The dealer distributes twenty cards to each person until each player has two stacks of ten cards (twenty cards total), facedown on the table. When players have their stacks, they turn over the top card on each stack and place it faceup on their pile. The remaining cards are placed in a stack in the middle of the table, forming the stock.

Determine your Hand and Foot. Choose which of your two piles you want to start playing with; this pile is called the Hand. The other pile is called the Foot, and you put it aside until you're done playing the Hand.

Points for Cards

4, 5, 6, 7, 8 = 5 points each
9, 10, J, Q, K = 10 points each
ACES = 20 points each
2s = 20 points each
JOKERS = 50 points each

> **NOTE** Jokers and 2s are wild cards, which means you can assign them any rank that you want to create a meld, although they maintain their point value even in melds.

3♣, 3♠ (BLACK) = –100 points
3♥, 3♦ (RED) = –300 points

> **NOTE** In this version, red 3s and black 3s cannot be melded; you can only discard them. These cards will give you negative points if they are in your possession when someone goes out, so try to discard them quickly.

Points for Groups of Cards

DIRTY PILES *(at least seven of the same-value cards with wild cards)* = 300 points each
CLEAN PILES *(at least seven of the same-value cards with no wild cards)* = 500 points each
WILD PILES *(at least seven wild cards)* = 1,500 points

BONUS FOR GOING OUT FIRST = 100 points

— Rules for Melds and Piles —

The object of Hand and Foot is to build *melds* (combinations of three cards) until they become *complete piles* (combinations of seven cards). This cheat sheet is helpful for beginners.

MELD REQUIREMENTS. A meld is a sequence of at least three cards or more all of the same rank (suit doesn't matter). Melds can be made with a mix of natural and wild cards.

MELD EXAMPLES

THREE-CARD CLEAN MELD: 4♣, 4♠, 4♥ (15 points)
THREE-CARD DIRTY MELD: 4♦, 4♦, 2♠ (40 points)
THREE-CARD WILD MELD: Joker, 2♠, 2♦ (70 points)

NOTE A dirty meld of three, four, or five cards can contain only one wild card. A dirty meld of six cards can contain only two wild cards.

PILE REQUIREMENTS. Melds that have seven cards are known as *complete piles*.

PILE EXAMPLES

SEVEN-CARD DIRTY PILE: Q♥, Q♠, Q♠, Q♣, Q♦, 2♥, Joker
(230 points)
SEVEN-CARD CLEAN PILE: Q♥, Q♥, Q♠, Q♠, Q♣, Q♣, Q♦
(370 points)
SEVEN-CARD WILD PILE: Joker, Joker, 2♦, 2♥, 2♥, 2♣, 2♣
(1,700 points)

NOTE A dirty pile can have no more than three wild cards.

Other Rules

No card may ever be taken out of a meld once it is formed.

During play, you can always add cards to your melds to build complete piles. However, you cannot add wild cards to an established meld.

A partnership cannot have two separate melds of cards in the same rank in progress at the same time. In other words, you must form a complete pile of 7s before laying down another meld with 7s.

When players achieve a complete pile, they often stack their cards and put a red card on top to indicate the pile is clean, a black card on top to indicate that the pile is dirty, or a wild card on top to indicate that the pile is wild.

Arrange your hand. Look at your cards and arrange them in terms of melds. You want to group three of a kind or more using natural cards and wild cards.

PLAYING YOUR TURN. The player to the dealer's left goes first. On your turn, you play as follows:

Draw two cards from the stock on your first turn (in this version, you cannot draw cards from the discard pile on your first turn).

On all subsequent turns, you may draw two cards from the stock or draw the top card and up to seven cards beneath it from the discard pile. The rules for drawing from the discard pile are as follows:

- The top card of the discard pile cannot be a 3.

- You must immediately meld this top card using two cards of the same rank that are *already* in your hand.

Lay down your first meld (opening). Putting down your first meld is called "opening." The first meld that you lay on the table must equal a minimum number of points. Each hand of the four hands played in this game has a different minimum opening requirement.

50 points for 1st hand
90 points for 2nd hand
120 points for 3rd hand
150 points for 4th hand

EXAMPLE Here are two scenarios for opening:

- The discard pile has a K♠. In your hand, you have a K♣ and a Joker. You can open. You show your K♣ and Joker and pick up the K♠ from the discard pile, laying it down together with your two cards to form a meld equaling 70 points (kings are 10 points each and Joker is 50 points).

- You pick up a 4♣ from the stock. You decide to lay down that 4♣ with a 4♣ and 2♥ from your hand to make one meld equal to 30 points. That is not enough to open but you also have a J♦, J♠, and 2♠ in your hand to form another meld equal to 40 points. By laying down both these melds, you have opened with two melds equaling 70 points.

Laying off. After you open, you can lay down as many melds from your hand as you'd like. If your partner opens first, you may also add cards to your partner's melds. Once one player opens, that player usually collects all the melds for the team in front of him.

You can only add cards to melds in your partnership and you can never take cards out of melds.

Playing the Foot. Once you're done playing cards in the Hand, you pick up your Foot and start playing those cards. If you happen to lay down cards and then discard the final card in your Hand, you then pick up your Foot but cannot start playing those cards until your next turn.

If, however, you lay down all your cards in your Hand and do not have a discard, you then pick up your Foot and continue playing as many of those cards as you can until you discard.

Discard a card. You complete your turn by throwing one card from your hand into the discard pile.

ENDING THE HAND. When one partner has no more cards to play, he can go out and the hand is over. You can go out by discarding your final card or adding it to a meld. There are a few requirements for going out:

- You must ask your partner if you can go out first.

- You cannot go out if your partner has not yet picked up his Foot.

- You cannot go out unless your partnership has at least two clean piles, two dirty piles, and one wild pile.

If the stock is depleted, it is possible to continue playing as long as each player is able and willing to take and meld the previous player's discard. As soon as one player wants to draw and is unable to, the hand is over. See the following scoring scenario if no one goes out.

SCORING

At the end of the hand, both teams add up the point value of their melds and piles.

The team that went out first adds 100 points to their score.

The team that did *not* go out tallies up the total point value of cards still in each player's hand and subtracts those points from the team score. Remember that you subtract 100 points for black 3s and 300 points for red 3s.

If no one goes out, both teams add up the point value of their melds and piles and subtract points for unmelded cards. Neither team gets the 100-point bonus.

Cards are all returned to the dealer and shuffled and the next hand starts. Remember that on round two both teams will need 90 points to open.

After all four hands are played, points are tallied and the highest score wins.

CANASTA

I n the world of card games, Canasta is relatively new. The game was invented in Uruguay in the 1940s. A few years after World War II, the Canasta craze swept the United States. In 1949, *Time* magazine reported that Canasta was all the rage: "This newest fad is a rip-roaring, high scoring game of the Rummy family. It combines the melding features of Pinochle, the building principle of Gin, and some of the partnership elements of Bridge. What a Canasta player needs most is endurance." *Canasta* is Spanish for basket, and it is thought to come from the small card tray that some people use to hold the two decks required to play the game.

RATING Challenging

PLAYERS 4 Players (two teams of 2). Partners sit across from each other.

DECK Two full decks of 52 cards with 2 Jokers per deck, all shuffled together.

RANKING Canasta is all about racking up points, so ranking doesn't come into the play of the game.

OBJECTIVE A typical game is played to 5,000 points.

SCORING See chart below.

◆——— Points for Cards ———◆

A = 20 points each
K, Q, J, 10, 9, 8 = 10 points each
7, 6, 5, 4, 3♠, 3♣ = 5 points each
3♥, 3♦ = 100 points each (all four red 3s = 800 points)
2s *(wild card)* = 20 points each
JOKERS *(wild card)* = 50 points each

Jokers and 2s are wild cards, which means you can assign them any rank that you want to create a meld, although they maintain their point value even in melds (see examples, page 84).

DIRTY *(or mixed)* **CANASTAS** = 300 points each
CLEAN *(or natural)* **CANASTAS** = 500 points each
GOING OUT = 100 points
GOING OUT CONCEALED = 200 points

◆——— Rules for Melds and Canastas ———◆

To win at Canasta, you are playing your hand to build *melds* and *canastas*.

MELD REQUIREMENTS. A meld is a sequence of at least three cards all of the same rank (suit doesn't matter). Melds can be made with a mix of natural and wild cards.

MELD EXAMPLES

THREE-CARD NATURAL MELD: 4♣, 4♠, 4♥ (15 points)
THREE-CARD MIXED MELD: 4♦, 4♦, 2♠ (40 points)

A three-card meld can have only one wild card (for example: 7♦, 2♠, Joker is not acceptable).

FOUR-CARD NATURAL MELD: 9♥, 9♣, 9♣, 9♦ (40 points)
FOUR-CARD MIXED MELD: 9♣, 9♥, Joker, 2♣ (90 points)

A four-card meld can have no more than two wild cards (for example: J♣, 2♥, Joker, 2♣ is not acceptable).

FIVE-CARD MIXED MELDS: 10♦, 10♥, 10♠, Joker, 2♠ (100 points)

A five-card meld or more can have no more than three wild cards (example: 10♦, 10♥, Joker, 2♠, 2♦ is unacceptable).

OTHER SPECIAL RULES. The 3♣ and 3♠ cannot be used in a meld unless you are going out. When you are going out, you can only create *natural* melds with the black 3s (you cannot include a wild card).

All melds must have at least two natural cards. No card may ever be taken out of a meld once it is formed.

CANASTA REQUIREMENTS. Melds that have seven cards or more are called canastas. As you and your partner play, one of your goals to create at least one canasta. Canastas score big points because you get to add together the point value for the canasta with the point values for the cards.

SEVEN-CARD MIXED CANASTA: Q♥, Q♠, Q♠, Q♣, 2♣, 2♥, Joker (430 points)
SEVEN-CARD CLEAN CANASTA: Q♥, Q♥, Q♠, Q♠, Q♣, Q♣, Q♦ (570 points)

A mixed canasta can have no more than three wild cards.

The maximum number of cards in a canasta is eleven because you can never have more than three wild cards in any meld. For example: 5♥, 5♥, 5♣, 5♣, 5♠, 5♠, 5♦, 5♦, 2♥, 2♠, Joker.

OTHER SPECIAL RULES. During play, you can always add cards to your canastas. If you have a mixed canasta of 5s and you draw a 5, then you can add it to your canasta.

You cannot add wild cards to an established canasta.

When players get a canasta, they often stack their cards and put a red card on top for natural or a black card on top for mixed.

HOW TO PLAY

DEAL THE CARDS. The dealer doles out eleven cards to each player, distributing one at a time. The remaining cards go into a pile in the middle called the stock. The top card is flipped over faceup and placed beside the stock to create the discard pile. If this card is a Joker or a 2 or a 3, another card is taken from the top and placed faceup on top of the first card. Cards are turned over onto the discard pile until the top card is not a 3, Joker, or 2.

Arrange your hand. Look at your cards and think how to arrange them in terms of melds. You want to group together three or more of a kind using natural cards and wild cards.

PLAYING YOUR TURN. The player to the dealer's left goes first. On your turn, you can either draw the top card from the stock or use the top card on the discard pile, and then play as follows:

If you draw a card from the stock, you have the following options. Discard that card immediately if you don't want it; put it into your hand and discard another card; use that card to lay down a meld with other cards from your hand; or add the card to a meld that your partner already has on the table.

If you want to use the card on top of the discard pile, you must take the whole discard pile AND you must be able to use the top card to lay down a meld (or add it to one of your partnership's melds on the table). After you have used this top card in a meld, you may incorporate the other cards from the discard pile into melds.

EXAMPLE Suppose there is a 10♣ on top of the discard pile with a 10♠ and 10♦ underneath. If you pick up this pile, you cannot use those three 10s to create a meld. You must add the 10♣ to a preexisting meld or create a new meld with the 10♣ and cards already in your hand. Once you have established the meld, you can then add the other 10s to it.

Lay down your first meld (opening). Putting down your first meld is called "opening." If you are the first player in your partnership to take a turn, the very first meld(s) that you lay down must equal a minimum of 50 points. If your partner goes first, he must meet the opening requirements, and then your first meld can be any point value.

EXAMPLE Here are two scenarios for opening:

- The discard pile has a K♠. In your hand, you have a K♣ and a Joker, worth 60 points. You can open. You show your K♣ and Joker and pick up the discard pile, laying the K♠ down together with those two cards to form a meld equaling 70 points (kings are 10 points each and the Joker is 50 points).

- You pick up a 4♣ from the stock. You decide to lay down that 4♣ with a 4♣ and 2♥ from your hand to make one meld equal to 30 points. That is not enough to open but you also have a J♦, J♠, and 2♠ in your hand to form another meld equal to 40 points. By laying down both these melds, you have opened with two melds equaling 70 points.

◆

OPENING REQUIREMENTS

◆

Opening requirements change as the game goes on. So when each new hand is dealt, you have to check your score and refer to these rules:

- If you and your partner have a score of **0 to 1,495,** you must lay down meld(s) of at least **50 points** to open.

- If you and your partner have a score of **1,500 to 2,995,** you must lay down meld(s) of at least **90 points** to open.

- If you and your partner have a score of **3,000 or more,** you must lay down meld(s) of at least **120 points** to open.

- As you play, you could lose enough points so that your score goes below zero. If you and your partner have a score of **less than 0,** you can open with any meld, which means **at least 15 points.**

Laying off. Once you open, you want to keep playing your cards to build melds and canastas. Sometimes, you will draw a card that you can add to a meld already on the table. You can add cards only to melds in your partnership and you can never take cards out of melds.

Discard the card. After you have drawn the top card or taken from the discard pile and then made as many melds as you want or added to melds, your turn is over and you must discard a card.

END THE HAND. A player goes out when he gets rid of all cards in his hand. But a player cannot go out unless the team has at least one canasta. The first player to go out earns the team an extra 100 points.

Going out with a "concealed hand" earns 200 points for the team. Going out "concealed" means that you have laid nothing on the table but you are able to play all your cards at once and go out. You may have a canasta in your hand or your partner may already have a canasta on the table.

Once a player goes out, each other player has to subtract the point value of the cards in his hand from the team's score. Then each team adds up all the points from the cards they have laid out in melds and canastas, making sure to count points for canastas made and red 3s (see Special Rules of Play, below, for 3s).

NOTE Before going out, it's customary to ask your partner, "May I go out?" Your partner may be holding some high point cards and so may advise you not to go out yet.

In rare cases, if the stock pile runs out before a player has gone out, play continues using the discard pile as stock. As long as each player can take the previous player's discard and meld it, play continues. As soon as a player cannot pick up the top card of the discard pile when the stock is exhausted, the game is over.

Once both teams are done tallying points, cards are returned to the deck and the new deal goes to the player to the left of the original dealer.

SPECIALS RULES OF PLAY

The Unique Power of 3s

BLACK 3s. If you discard a black 3, it blocks the discard pile for the next player (he cannot pick it up). He must pick the top card from the stock, create or add to any melds, and then discard. After his turn, the discard pile is unblocked for the next player.

Remember, black 3s cannot be used in a meld unless you are going out, and you can form natural melds only with your black 3s (no wild cards).

RED 3s. These cards give you bonus points. When you are dealt a red 3, you simply set it faceup by your side and the dealer must give you another card to complete your hand. If you draw a red 3 during the play, you must set it faceup by your side and draw another card.

A red 3 immediately gives you 100 points. If you and your partner end up with all four red 3s, you score double their usual value for 800 points. Note that red 3s do not count toward opening. In the rare case that a red 3 is in the discard pile, the player who gets the pile does not replace that red 3 with another card.

FREEZING THE PILE. We already know that the black 3 freezes the discard pile for the subsequent player. Also, if your partnership does not have a meld or can't create a meld, the discard pile is frozen to you. But there are more ways that the pile can be frozen:

- When a player discards a wild card (a 2 or a Joker) in the pile.

- At the beginning of the hand, if the dealer turns over a wild card to create the discard pile, the first player cannot pick up that wild card (he must draw a card from the stock).

- At the beginning of a hand, if the dealer turns over a red 3 to create the discard pile, the first player cannot pick up that red 3 (he must draw a card from the stock).

You cannot pick up the discard pile in any of these cases unless you have at least two natural cards *in your hand* to make a meld with the top discard.

EXAMPLE **PLAYER 1** discards a 2♣, freezing the pile.

PLAYER 2 has to pick up the top card from the stock because the discard pile is frozen. Player 2 discards a 6♥.

PLAYER 3 already has five 6s melded on the table, but he has no 6s in his hand. He cannot pick up the discard pile. Player 3 picks from the stock and discards a 5♦.

PLAYER 4 has two 5s in his hand. These two natural cards match the top card on the discard pile, so he picks up the entire pile, starts a new meld with the three 5s, and discards a card (starting a new unfrozen discard pile).

If you play a wild card and freeze the pile, place the card perpendicular in the discard pile so that everyone knows the pile is frozen.

As a strategy, you may want to freeze the discard pile when your partnership doesn't have many canastas, but the opposing team does. Your team may be holding a lot of cards and is more likely to unfreeze the pile. Meanwhile you may prevent the other team from getting more points.

◇◇◇

STRATEGY

- **Don't have too few cards in your hand.** Putting too many down on the table and not keeping enough cards in your hand can limit your play. Opening with small melds can help keep cards in your hand.

- **Try to accumulate pairs.** The more possible pairs you have in your hand, the more likely you are able to pick up the discard pile. Picking up the discard pile can help you get points.

- **Be careful to play the high cards.** You don't want to be stuck with Jokers, aces, and 2s in your hand at the end. Try to get a sense of whether your opponent may be going out soon and play your high cards.

- **Don't hesitate to use a wild card to block.** It's tempting to keep a wild card in your hand, but played strategically the wild card may be able to stop an opponent who is ahead. Your block could also keep an opponent from opening.

EXAMPLE Your team has just 1,200 points while the opposing team has 3,200 points. Your team can open more easily with 50 points as opposed to their 120 points needed to open. Your team may be able to form a canasta and even go out before the opposing team gets a meld on the table. Freezing the pile has the potential to make it harder for them to pick up the discard pile and get the cards they need to open.

◇◇◇

SCORING

When one player goes out, the hand ends and each team has to total their scores.

To arrive at your score:

- Add up the point value of your canastas

- Add up the point value of your melds

- Add the bonus points for your red 3s

- Subtract the total point value of any cards that you were holding when the hand ended

A partnership combines both players' scores to arrive at the team score.

Typically, the team that reaches 5,000 points wins the game, but you can lower this requirement if you want to play a shorter game.

Cool Fact

When James Bond first meets Goldfinger, the villain is cheating at a game of Canasta, receiving information about an opponent's hand through a bogus hearing aid.

IV

The concept of bidding can be confounding to a novice card player. Bidding games require you to declare how many tricks you *think* you can win before you start playing your hand. *How are you supposed to know this?* At first, placing a bid may feel like a shot in the dark, but you will get better at assessing your hand with time.

SPADES

S pades started in the Midwestern United States in the late 1930s, and it quickly grew in popularity during World War II. As a trick-taking game, it has roots in Whist and is related to Oh Hell!, Hearts, and Bridge. You can find quite a few computer versions of Spades online.

RATING Easy

PLAYERS 4 players. In this version, each person plays and scores individually, rather than in teams of 2.

DECK One full 52 card deck.

CARD RANKING Standard ranking, aces high.

OBJECTIVE To be the first person to score a minimum of 500 points.

<><><><><><><><><><><><><><><><><><><><><><><><><><><><><><><><><><><><><><><><><>

HOW TO PLAY

DEAL THE CARDS. The dealer distributes thirteen cards to each player, one at a time.

Placing a bid. Since each player holds thirteen cards, you will play thirteen times (tricks) in one hand. Before you play a hand, each player bids how many tricks she *thinks* she can win, based on the cards in her possession. To win a trick, you must play either (a) the highest card in the leading suit or (b) the highest trump card (spades).

> **EXAMPLE** You have been dealt the following hand:

7♥, A♥, 2♣, 4♣, 5♣, 10♣, J♣, 3♦, 4♦, 5♦, 2♠, 4♠, 8♠

You may want to make a conservative bid that you can win two tricks, because you hold two very high-ranking cards (the A♥ and the J♣), plus three trump cards (2♠, 4♠, 8♠).

If your hand has mostly low-ranking cards, you may bid *nil* (that you won't win any tricks in this round).

If you have been dealt mostly high-ranking cards—including

high-ranking trumps—you may bid to *shoot the moon*, or win all thirteen tricks.

TAKING TRICKS. The player sitting to the left of the dealer (the eldest) plays first. She plays a card, establishing the leading suit. The leading card can be any card *except* a spade. Spades cannot lead a trick until they are "broken"—that is, until a player has no cards in the leading suit *or* no other cards besides spades in her hand.

You must follow suit if you can. If you can't follow suit, you may play a trump card (a spade) or any other card (which means you won't win this trick). The winner of the trick (the person with the highest ranking card in the leading suit, or the highest trump card) clears the table—keeping the cards separate from her playing hand. The winner plays the leading card for the next trick.

EXAMPLE

Eldest	Player 2	Player 3	Dealer
10♥	K♥	7♥	6♦

In this case, the eldest establishes hearts as the leading suit with a 10♥, and Player 2 wins the trick with a K♥.

Eldest	Player 2	Player 3	Dealer
8♣	9♣	3♠	5♣

In this case, the eldest establishes the leading suit with the 8♣, but Player 3 wins the trick with a trump card, 3♠.

END THE HAND. When all thirteen tricks have been played—and everyone's hand is empty—the scores are tallied. Continue to deal new hands until the first player reaches 500 points—and wins!

◇◇

SCORING

Points are awarded for meeting or exceeding your bid for each round.

If you bid that you would win two tricks and succeed, you get 20 points (10 × a bid of 2).

If you bid that you would win two tricks and succeed in winning 3, you score 21 points (1 extra point for the extra trick, which is called an *overtrick*).

NOTE Be careful about winning too many overtricks. Each time you accumulate 10 overtricks, 100 points are deducted from your score.

If you fail to meet your bid, you lose ten times the bid value. So, if you declared that you would win three tricks, your score would be –30 points (–10 × a bid of 3).

If you bid *nil* and succeed (by deliberately *not* winning any tricks), you score 100 points. If you bid *nil* and fail (by actually winning a trick, in spite of your intention to lose all), you score –100 points.

If you *shoot the moon* and succeed, you score 200 points. If you *shoot the moon* and fail, your score will be –200 points.

OH HELL!

This is a classic trick-taking game that is best for three or more players. It's often a fun game to play with large groups and is popular at family gatherings and parties. There are no partnerships—it's every man for himself. The game was very popular in the early 1900s. It gets its name because it can make you curse a lot—so more conservative players call it Oh Pshaw! or Oh Heck! or Oh Darn! The game is also known as Elevator Whist, Up the River, German Bridge, and Blackout.

RATING Medium

PLAYERS 2 or more players (good for large groups).

DECK One full deck without Jokers for up to 6 players. Two decks for 7 or more players.

RANKING Standard ranking with ace high.

OBJECTIVE To win the most points by winning the number of tricks you bid.

◇◇◇

HOW TO PLAY

DEAL THE CARDS. Hands grow progressively bigger in Oh Hell! The dealer passes out one card to each player for the first hand; two cards for the second hand; three cards for the third hand; and so on.

Determine the trump. After each hand is dealt, the dealer flips over the card on top of the deck and shows it to all of the players. The suit of that card sets trump for the hand. The card is placed back in the deck, and the deck is set aside until the next hand is dealt.

Placing a bid. Starting to the dealer's left, each player must make a bid. Your bid is essentially your prediction of how many tricks you expect to win with your hand. In Oh Hell!, you have to win your bid *exactly* to get points.

You can bid from zero to the number of cards in your hand. When you bid zero, you are predicting that you will not win any tricks.

On the first hand, each player gets one card, so each player can either bid 1 or zero.

EXAMPLE The trump card is 6♣ and there are three players holding the following cards:

PLAYER 1 has A♦.

She gets to play the leading card for the first trick, but her card is not in the trump suit. Still, she thinks her high ace may win the trick, so she bids one.

PLAYER 2 has 4♣.

She thinks she has a chance to win because she has a trump card. But the rank of the trump is low, so someone could beat her with a higher trump card. She decides to go for it and bids one.

PLAYER 3 (the dealer) has 10♠.

She has a high card, but she has no idea what the leading suit will be. Player 1 could lead with a spade, but the 10♠ might not be high enough to win the trick. She bids zero, thinking she won't win any tricks.

TAKING TRICKS. Play begins to the dealer's left. Following the general rules for trick-taking, the first player puts down a card and the rest of the players must follow suit. If you can't follow suit, you can play a trump card (trump is the most powerful suit in the hand and beats any other suit) or you can play another card (which means you won't win the trick).

The highest trump card wins the trick. If no one plays a trump card, the highest card of the leading suit takes the trick. Whoever wins the trick will play the first card for the next trick (regardless of whether this player has won her bid).

ENDING A HAND (and beginning a new hand). After all of the tricks have been played, the cards are collected and shuffled. The deal rotates left, and the new dealer distributes two cards per player (the dealer does not pick a new trump card for each hand).

Play continues until cards can no longer be dealt equally among the players. Some people eliminate the trump suit for the final hand. The number of hands played is usually as follows:

3 PLAYERS = 15 hands
4 PLAYERS = 13 hands
5 PLAYERS = 10 hands
6 PLAYERS = 8 hands
7 PLAYERS = 7 hands

SCORING

One person keeps score for all players. You get 1 point for each trick that you take—plus 10 points for getting the exact number you bid. If you don't win the exact number of tricks you bid, you don't get any points. After all the cards are played, points are all tallied and the highest score wins.

EXAMPLE Here are the scores earned by the players in the previous bidding example, after the trick is played:

PLAYER 1 leads with the A♦.

PLAYER 2 puts down her 4♣.

PLAYER 3 puts down her 10♠.

PLAYER 2 wins with her trump. She gets 11 points (1 point for winning the trick and 10 points for getting her bid correct). She collects the three cards and places her trick by her side.

PLAYER 3 also wins 10 points for predicting her bid of zero correctly.

PLAYER 1 bid 1 trick and didn't win any tricks so she gets 0 points.

The player with the highest score after all the hands are played is the winner.

NAPOLEON

Dating back to the late 1800s in England, this game is named after the famous French emperor. It is also called Napoleon Euchre or simply Nap. The game uses distinct bidding terms—Wellington and Blücher—as a tribute to the two generals who defeated Napoleon at the Battle of Waterloo, and Nap, referring to the great dictator himself. This game provides a simple introduction to the world of bidding. Although not as popular as it once was, it is still played, predominantly in parts of southern England and Scotland. People usually play for small stakes. (Note: There is also a card game that originates in Japan called Napoleon or Japanese Napoleon, but it is completely different from this game.)

RATING Medium

PLAYERS 4–6 players

DECK One full deck of 52 cards without Jokers. Plus chips or pennies that players either win from or pay out to other players. You might start with 20 such tokens per player.

RANKING Standard ranking with the ace always high.

OBJECTIVE To win tricks and score points. The game is often played to 25 points, but you may want to go higher with more people playing (50 points may be better for 4 people).

◇◇

HOW TO PLAY

DEAL THE CARDS. Starting to his left, the dealer distributes cards in alternating batches of three and then two until each player has five cards.

Placing a bid. Each player looks at his hand, deciding if he will be able to win tricks with his cards. Beginning to the dealer's left, each player has a chance to place a bid or pass. A bid is a prediction of the number of tricks you think you can win with your hand.

In Napoleon, each successive player's bid must be higher than the previous, up to a bid of 5. If you cannot make a higher bid than the previous player, you must pass.

POSSIBLE BIDS, RANKING FROM LOW TO HIGH:

- **You can bid that you will win three tricks.** Winning this bid = 3 points.

- **You can bid that you will lose all five tricks.** Essentially, you can win by losing. The bid is called Mis, short for Misère. It falls between a bid of three and a bid of four. So bidding Mis beats a bid of three but can be beaten by a bid of four.

- **You can bid that you will win four tricks.** Winning this bid = 4 points.

- **You can bid that you will win all five tricks.** This is called Nap. Winning Nap = 5 points.

- **If the player before you bids Nap, you can still bid that you will win five tricks.** This wipes out the previous player's bid of Nap. This is called Wellington. Winning Wellington = 10 points.

- **If the player before you bids Wellington, you can still bid that you will win five tricks.** This wipes out the previous player's bid of Wellington. This is called Blücher. Winning Blücher = 20 points.

There is no bonus or penalty for winning tricks beyond your bid.

If you fall short of your bid, you must subtract that bid from your score (or if you are playing with chips, you must pay out to the winner the number of chips equaling your bid).

The bidding ends at Blücher and then playing the hand begins.

There is only one round of bidding. If all players pass, the hand is dead. All cards are returned to the dealer, the deck is reshuffled, and a fresh hand is dealt.

EXAMPLE **PLAYER 1** has J♣, 9♣, Q♦, 6♥, J♠.

He thinks that the two jacks and queen give him a shot at winning three tricks. But calling trump is a problem, since his hand isn't really dominant in any one suit. Still, he takes a risk and bids 3.

PLAYER 2 has 10♥, 4♥, 10♠, 7♣, 3♦.

His hand isn't strong in any one suit, so calling trump would be tricky. He also doesn't have any high-ranking cards, so he passes.

PLAYER 3 has A♠, 7♠, 5♠, 4♠, J♥.

He has four spades, so setting spades as the trump would be an easy call. He thinks that if he plays his cards right, his trump cards could win (this is a little risky, since his trump cards aren't very high, aside from the A♠). He decides to bid 4.

PLAYER 4 has 10♦, 6♦, 2♦, 5♥, 3♠.

He has three diamonds, but holds mostly low-ranking cards. He was considering bidding Mis (and attempting to lose all five tricks), but Player 3 has outbid him. He passes.

TAKING TRICKS. The highest bidder gets to play the first card of the hand, putting it in the middle of the table. The suit of this card sets trump for the entire hand (all five tricks that will be played).

You must follow suit if you can. With the first trick, your only option is to play a trump suit or another suit, which will not win the trick. The trick is won by the player with the highest trump card.

The winner of first trick gets to play the lead card for the next trick. Again, you must follow suit or play a trump card; if you have neither, you can play a card of any suit (which means that you can't win that trick). Trump cards beat any other suit, and if two players put down a trump card, the highest trump card takes the trick.

EXAMPLE Player 3 won the bid and goes first.

	Player 3	Player 4	Player 1	Player 2	
1st trick	A♠	3♠	J♠	10♠	(Player 3 wins)
2nd trick	7♠	2♦	6♥	3♦	(Player 3 wins)
3rd trick	5♠	5♥	9♣	4♥	(Player 3 wins)
4th trick	4♠	6♦	J♣	7♠	(Player 3 wins)
5th trick	J♥	10♦	Q♦	10♥	(Player 3 wins)

ENDING THE HAND. The hand is over after all five cards are played and five tricks have been won. The players score their hand and the deal rotates left (all cards are collected, reshuffled, and the next hand is dealt).

◇◇

SCORING

The sample hand above would be scored as follows:

Player 1 failed to meet his bid of 3: his score is –3 (or he pays 3 chips to the winner).

Player 2 passed: his score is 0 (no chips paid to the winner).

Player 3 met his bid of four tricks: his score is 4 (or he wins chips from all players who don't make their bid).

Player 4 passed: his score is 0 (no chips paid to the winner).

The game is usually played to 25 points (the first player to reach that score wins).

Remember, you can score points only for winning bids, *not* for winning hands. So, if Player 2 (who passed) actually ended up winning a trick, his score would still be 0.

Likewise, you don't score extra points for exceeding your bid (so Player 3 does not get an extra point for winning five tricks instead of four.)

You aren't penalized for exceeding your bid, which makes this game easier for players who are new to bidding.

CINCH

In Euchre, the jack of the trump suit takes on an important role. In Cinch, the 5 of the trump suit is the most special card. Also called High Five or Double Pedro, Cinch may get its name from *cinco*, the Spanish word for five, or *cinq*, which is French for five. Others believe the game's name comes from its common meaning "to secure," as with a belt, because players in the game want to secure the tricks. The game supposedly emerged in the western United States in the early 1900s.

RATING Moderately Challenging

PLAYERS 4 players—two teams of 2.

DECK One full deck of 52 cards without Jokers.

RANKING Ace high to 2 low with a unique twist. The 5 in the trump suit is called the high Pedro and the 5 of the suit that is the same color as trump becomes the low Pedro. As in Euchre, the low Pedro leaves its suit and becomes a card in the trump suit.

EXAMPLE If hearts are the trump suit, the ranking for hearts is A♥, K♥, Q♥, J♥, 10♥, 9♥, 8♥, 7♥, 6♥, 5♥ (high Pedro), 5♦ (low Pedro), 4♥, 3♥, 2♥. The diamonds suit will then rank A♦, K♦, Q♦, J♦, 10♦, 9♦, 8♦, 7♦, 6♦, 4♦, 3♦, 2♦ without the 5♦. All other suits are ranked normally.

OBJECTIVE To win tricks that contain point-scoring cards. The first team to score 51 points wins.

SCORING To decide how to bid, you have to know the point system for the game up front. Only five cards score points.

⟶ Points for Cards ⟵

HIGH PEDRO *(5 of trump)* = 5 points
LOW PEDRO *(5 of the same color as trump)* = 5 points
ACE OF TRUMP = 1 point
JACK OF TRUMP = 1 point
10 OF TRUMP = 1 point
2 OF TRUMP = 1 point

HOW TO PLAY

DEAL THE CARDS. Dealer gives out nine cards per player, dealing three cards at a time.

Placing a bid. In most bidding games, you start by bidding (or predicting) how many tricks you and your partner think you will win. In Cinch, however, you bid the number of *points* you think you and your partner will win after playing the six tricks that make up a hand. If you win the bid—that is, make the highest bid out of all the players, you get to declare trump.

The minimum bid is 1 and the maximum bid is 14—or all the possible points that could be scored with one hand. So when you bid, you're not only thinking, "Can my partnership win the trick," but "Is there a strong chance that we will win tricks with points?"

Starting to the dealer's left, each player makes a bid. Each bid must top the preceding bid or the player can pass. If all players pass, cards are returned to the deck, shuffled, and the dealer gives out a fresh new hand to each player.

EXAMPLE You have been dealt the following hand and you need to decide what to bid.

K♠, Q♠, J♠, 6♠, 4♠, 8♥, 5♥, 2♥, 4♦

You have five spades, which means that if you win this bid, you'll want to declare spades as the trump. Four of your spades are ranked higher than 5, which means that you have a shot at winning the high-scoring 5♠ or 5♣ with any of those cards. You also think that your 4♠ could win the 2♠ and get you a point. Your J♠ will score you a point if your team can keep it by winning the trick.

You start bidding at 6, thinking you will at least keep the J♠ and win either the 5♠ or 5♣ (worth 5 points). You think that you have the potential to win 12 points, so if you get into a bidding war with another player, you decide that a bid of 12 will be your limit.

Determining the trump. Again, the player who makes the highest bid gets to determine the trump. Trump is the most powerful suit of the hand and trump cards beat any other suit, so obviously, if your hand is heavy in a particular suit, you'll want to make that suit as the trump.

Discard and replace cards. After the highest bidder names trump, each player discards all cards in his hands *except* the trump suits. Remember that the 5 of the same color as trump (low Pedro) is now a trump card and should not be discarded.

Then the dealer gives each player back enough cards so each player has only six cards instead of the original nine. The discarded cards are out of play. Here are your options for replacing cards:

- If you have no trump in all nine cards, you give back all nine and receive six new cards.

- If you have more than six trump cards in your hand, you decide which trump cards you're discarding and show the other players. These cards are all out of play.

The dealer's advantage. The dealer also discards his non-trump cards, but instead of blindly dealing new cards to himself, he has the privilege to "rob the pack." He can look through the deck and take whatever cards left in the pack that he likes—trump or otherwise— until he has six cards in his hand.

Why wouldn't the dealer want to take a trump card? If the dealer's team is not the bid-winner and he sees point-scoring trump cards in the deck, he can hedge that it will be difficult for his opponents to win their bid if these cards don't come into play.

TAKING TRICKS. The high bidder plays the first card and establishes the suit for that trick. Going to the left of the high bidder, each player must follow suit if possible, or play a trump card, or any other card. Each trick is won by the highest card of the leading suit or the highest trump card; no other card can win a trick.

ENDING THE HAND. After six tricks are played, the hand is over. The teams tally their points (see example below). The deal rotates to the left.

EXAMPLE Here is how a hand could play out after the bidding and discarding has taken place.

You are dealt the following hand: K♠, Q♠, J♠, 6♠, 4♠, 8♥, 5♥, 2♥, 4♦.

You start the bidding process with a bid of 6 and win with a bid of 10. You declare spades as trump.

You trade in your four non-trump cards (8♥, 5♥, 2♥, 4♦), which means that you need one new card from the dealer to achieve a final hand of six cards. You are dealt a 3♣.

After exchanging the other two players' discards, the dealer finalizes her own hand.

In this hand, the dealer has no trump cards (no spades). So she trades in all her cards and gets to rob the deck of six cards of her choice.

She decides to leave the 10♠ in the deck, which potentially deprives the other team of a point. She selects the 9♠, 8♠ (thinking she might win tricks with them) and takes A♦, Q♦, 5♦, Q♥. The ace and two queens give her high, potential trick-winning cards. There were no other good cards to choose so she took the 5♦ to finish her hand.

Each player's final hand is as follows:

YOUR HAND: K♠, Q♠, J♠, 6♠, 4♠, 3♣
DEALER'S PARTNER: 5♠, 5♣, 2♣, A♣, 7♦, 6♦
YOUR PARTNER: 7♠, 3♠, 2♠, A♠, J♦, 4♥
DEALER: 9♠, 8♠, A♦, Q♦, 5♦, Q♥

With these hands, you can see that in this case the bid-winning team is in a strong position. Here's how the hand could play out:

You	Dealer's Partner	Your Partner	Dealer	
K♠	5♠	7♠	9♠	(your team wins 5 points)
Q♠	5♣	A♠	8♠	(your team wins 5 points)
J♠	2♣	2♠	5♦	(your team wins 2 points)
6♠	6♦	3♠	Q♥	(no points scored)
4♠	7♦	4♥	Q♦	(no points scored)
3♣	A♣	J♦	A♦	(no points scored)

Your team wins a total of 12 points, which means that you've met your bid of 10. The other team scores 0.

If for some reason the opposing team had won 1 point, your team would have still made its bid, but your score would be 12, minus any points gained by the other team. Your final score for the hand would be 11.

◇◇◇

SCORING

Both teams tally the points they have won after playing the six tricks in a hand.

If the bid-winning team makes its bid (wins the points it predicted it would win or more), then it scores the points it has won minus points won by the opposing team. So, although it is rare, you could meet your bid but still end up with negative points if the other team wins some high-scoring cards in their tricks.

If you are the bid-winning team and you do not make your bid, you are penalized.

The opposing team automatically gets 14 points added to their score plus the number of points that your team fell short of its bid.

The first team to reach 51 points wins.

PINOCHLE

Derived from the nineteenth-century French game Bezique, Pinochle, sometimes called Pinocle or Penucle, was developed on the East Coast of America in the 1850s. Some say it also derives from the German game called Skat and the Swiss/German game Binokel, which was a version of Bezique. Some say the name Binokel relates to binocular and refers to the fact that you have two of each card in a Pinochle deck.

Points for Cards

Melding Points

RUNS

A, 10, K, Q, J OF TRUMP *(called a run)* = 15 points
A, A, 10, 10, K, K, Q, Q, J, J OF TRUMP *(a double run—this is very rare)* = 150
A, 10, K, K, Q, J OF TRUMP *(a run with an extra king)* = 19
A, 10, K, Q, Q, J OF TRUMP *(a run with an extra queen)* = 19
A, 10, K, K, Q, Q, J OF TRUMP *(a run with an extra king and queen)* = 23

> **NOTE** Runs must have trump to score points. If you win the bid, you get to declare trump. So if you see you have a run in your hand, it will help you figure out how much to bid.

MARRIAGES

K Q TRUMP *(the royal marriage)* = 4 points
K Q NON-TRUMP *(both of same suit but not trump)* = 2 points
K AND Q OF ALL FOUR SUITS *(or a marriage of every suit, called a Round Robin or Round House)* = 24 points

FOUR OF A KIND, ONE FROM EACH SUIT

A♥, A♠, A♦, A♣ *(called aces around)* = 10 points
K♥, K♠, K♦, K♣ *(called kings around)* = 8 points
Q♥, Q♠, Q♦, Q♣ *(called queens around)* = 6 points
J♥, J♠, J♦, J♣ *(called jacks around)* = 4 points

In the rare case you get all 8 of any of a kind, you add a zero to the points:

ALL ACES *(double aces around)* = 100 points
ALL KINGS *(double kings around)* = 80 points
ALL QUEENS *(double queens around)* = 60 points
ALL JACKS *(double jacks around)* = 40 points

PINOCHLE

Q♠ AND J♦ PLAYED TOGETHER IS CALLED PINOCHLE = 4 points
TWO Q♠S AND TWO J♦S PLAYED IS CALLED A DOUBLE PINOCHLE =
30 points

Note that you can have a pinochle built off of a marriage or run.

EXAMPLE ◀ If trump is spades and you have the run (A♠, 10♠, K♠, Q♠, J♠) and you hold the J♦, you get points for the run and the pinochle. Or if you have a marriage of K♠, Q♠, and the J♦, you get points for the marriage and the pinochle.

9 OF TRUMP (the lowest trump card called the dix and pronounced *deece*) = 1 point

Trick Points

You will also get points for winning tricks that have "point" cards.

A, 10, K each score 1 point.

9, Q, and J do not give you any points.

It doesn't matter if the card is from the trump suit or not.

There are 24 total points you can potentially win in these counter cards.

You win 1 more point if you win the final trick.

RATING Challenging

PLAYERS 4 players playing in partnerships (2 teams of 2 players). There are other versions, but this is how the game is most commonly played.

DECK A special pinochle deck of 48 cards (which you can make or buy). To make a pinochle deck, you need to take two cards of every denomination from two decks, from aces through 9s. So you have two A♥s, two A♠s, two A♦s, two A♣s, two K♥s, etc. All other cards are not in play.

RANKING Pinochle has its unique ranking that you have to get accustomed to. From highest to lowest, ranking is A, 10, K, Q, J, 9. So the 10 jumps up to be the second highest rank card.

OBJECTIVE Games are usually played to 250 points, so the overall goal is for your team to win the most points.

SCORING In the first phase of the game, you score points by forming melds with the cards in your hand. In the second phase of the game you score by winning tricks that include special point cards. Ideally, each player should have a copy of the points for cards cheat sheet (see pages 118–119) in front of them while playing.

◇◇

HOW TO PLAY

DEAL THE CARDS. Dealer distributes all the cards, twelve to each player. It's common to deal to the left, three cards at a time.

Arrange your hand. Most people begin by arranging their cards in terms of suits, but you also get points for specific melds of cards of the same rank.

Placing a bid. Before playing any cards, each player must bid (essentially predict) how many points he thinks his team will win. Refer to the scoring cheat sheet (pages 118–119) to evaluate the cards in your hand and estimate the possible points you and your partner could win.

In this version, the player to the dealer's left always starts with a minimum bid of 15. Then, each player goes around the table bidding at least 1 point more or passing. You can raise the bid by more than 1 point if you like. If everyone passes, the dealer automatically has to take the bid at 15.

Often, a player from each partnership winds up bidding back and forth, trying to win the bid, but you should only bid up to the point that you feel you have a reasonable chance of winning.

Determining the trump. If you win the bid, then you get to decide the trump for the hand.

EXAMPLE Suppose you're holding A♥, 10♥, K♥, Q♥, J♥

As you look at your hand, you have to think: "Okay, my partner and I will have two ways to score: (a) in the beginning, by melding cards in my hand, and (b) later in the game, by winning tricks with 'point' cards."

If you win the bid and declare hearts the trump, you will have a run worth 15 points.

You're also likely to win a few tricks. There are 25 possible points that can be won in the trick-taking part of the game. You estimate that you can win roughly half of these points, so you start the bid with 27 (15 melding points plus 12 points from tricks).

The next player may not have a strong hand, so he may pass.

Your partner knows from your bid that you have a strong hand, so he says pass.

The dealer has a strong hand too so he ups the bid to 28. You say 29. Dealer says 30. You are still hopeful and say 31. At that high of a bid, the dealer bows out and you've won the bid.

Why do you want to win the bid?

- If you win the bid, you get to declare trump and trump can win you more points.

- If you win the bid, you and your partner are allowed to exchange four cards from each other's hands, which increases your partnership's chances of getting higher-scoring melds and marriages.

- If you win the bid, you play the first card—giving you an opportunity to control the play of the game.

What if you can't make your bid? If you do not score at least the amount of points you bid at the beginning of the hand, you lose big. So you want to be fairly confident that you will make your bid.

Passing cards. If you win the bid, your partner immediately passes you four cards facedown and you put those cards in your hand. Then you pass your partner four cards facedown. (These cards can include cards your partner has just passed you.) This is advantageous because you have declared trump and your partner can slide you trump cards that might give you a run. You can slide your partner cards that might give him a "marriage" (see scoring possibilities on pages 118–119). The non-bidding team *does not* trade cards.

SHOW YOUR MELDS. Now, all players make the first real play of the game: showing melds. You look at your hand in terms of the melding points above and lay down on the table only the combinations that score points.

> **EXAMPLE** You win the bid and decide to declare clubs as the trump.

You choose this suit because clubs will give you the highest melding points, using the cards in your hand.

You lay down your hand: K♣, Q♣, J♥, J♠, J♦, J♣, 9♣

This scores your team 4 points for a royal marriage (K♣, Q♣), four jacks is 4 points, and 9♣ is the dix in this case, so you earn 1 point.

The scorekeeper writes down the points scored by each team for their combined melds.

Decide if you are still "on board." At this stage, if the bid-winning team thinks it has no chance of reaching its bid, it can end the hand before proceeding to the trick-taking portion of the hand. This is called "not being on board."

If your bid is higher than your meld points plus 25 (the possible trick-taking points), then you have no chance of reaching your bid—you are "not on board." In this case, the opposing team scores the points from the melds it had laid down, and the bidding team subtracts their original bid from its score. The hand ends there.

> **EXAMPLE** Say you won the bid with 35 points and declared clubs as trump.

In this melding stage, you lay down K♠ and Q♠ for 4 points, 9♠ for 1 point (5 points total).

Your partner lays down two non-trump marriages—K♥ and Q♥ and K♦ and Q♦. That equals 4 points.

At this point, you know you have a guaranteed 9 points. However, you would need to win 26 more points to meet your bid and the most you can win in trick-taking is 25 points. At this point, it is better to get 35 points knocked off your score for declaring that you are "not on board" than it would be to keep playing this hand.

Shooting the moon. One more possible option to keep in mind: This is a rare case, but, once all the melds are scored and before trick-taking starts, a bid-winner can declare "shoot the moon." This means the team intends to win every trick. If the bid-winning team succeeds, it gets 25 extra points. If not, they subtract an extra 25 points from their score when points are finally tallied. It's fairly difficult to shoot the moon. You may want to leave this rule out when you first start to play, but it can be fun to include later on as you master the game.

TAKING TRICKS. Whoever wins the bid leads the trick-taking stage of the game. The object now is to win as many aces, 10s, and kings as possible to get points. After scoring the melds, all the players take up their cards again. The bid-winner plays the leading card. Each player must follow suit if he can.

If you cannot follow suit, you can play a trump card or another suit (this card cannot win the trick). The highest card of the leading suit will win the trick, unless a trump card is played. If two trump cards are played, the highest trump card wins the trick. If two identical cards are played that could win the trick, the first card played of those two wins it.

After all twelve tricks are played, the trick-taking points are tallied and added to the meld points to arrive at the final score for the hand.

EXAMPLE Trump is ♦

YOU: A♦
DEALER'S PARTNER: A♦
YOUR PARTNER: K♦
DEALER: Q♦

When two cards of the same suit are played that could win the trick, the win goes to the first winning card played. So you collect that trick and your team scores 3 points for taking the aces and the king. The Q♦ does not have a point value.

ENDING THE HAND. After the scores are tallied from both the melding and trick-taking portions of the game, the cards are returned to the deck and the deal goes to the next player to the left.

◇◇

SCORING

If your team was the bid-winner and you reach or surpass your bid, you keep all the points your team earned during trick-taking and melding.

If you are the bid-winner and do not reach your bid, you "go set," which means you lose big. You do not score your points taken in tricks. You do not score your points taken in melds. *And* you subtract the points you bid. So, if you do not win the hand after winning the bid, the penalty is huge.

Whether the bid-winning team reaches its bid or not, the non-bid-winning team keeps its points, unless that team does not score at least 1 point during the trick-taking part of the game. Then the non-bid-winning team loses its melded points as well—but it would keep any point from a dix, the lowest trump card.

For example, let's say that Team A bid 24 and won.

In melding, Team A had four jacks for 4 points, a royal marriage for 4 points, and then they won 14 points in tricks. With a total score of 22 points, Team A did not reach its bid, so the team scores –24.

Team B had one non-trump marriage of a K and Q for 2 points, and 9 of trump for 1 point. They also won 10 points in tricks (as well as 1 bonus point for winning the final trick). Team B keeps all its points for a score of 14.

The first team to reach 250 points wins.

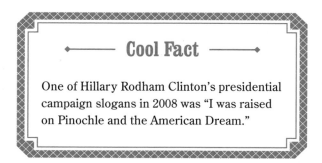

Cool Fact

One of Hillary Rodham Clinton's presidential campaign slogans in 2008 was "I was raised on Pinochle and the American Dream."

CARD GAME COCKTAILS

SEVEN OF SPADES

1 ounce amaretto
2 ounces whiskey
2 ounces Coca-Cola

Fill a Tom Collins glass with ice. Pour in all of the ingredients and stir well. Garnish with a maraschino cherry, if desired.

QUEEN OF HEARTS

1 ounce gin
1 ounce strawberry juice
$\frac{1}{4}$ ounce red wine infused with
    simple syrup
Champagne

Combine the gin, juice, and wine in a cocktail shaker half-filled with ice. Shake well and strain into a martini glass. Top with champagne.

CASINO ROYALE

2 ounces gin
$\frac{1}{2}$ ounce lemon juice
1 teaspoon maraschino cherry
    liqueur
Dash of orange bitters
1 egg yolk

Combine ingredients in a cocktail shaker half-filled with ice. Shake well and strain into a sour glass.

WHIST COCKTAIL

$1\frac{1}{2}$ ounces rum
$\frac{1}{2}$ ounce applejack
$\frac{3}{4}$ ounce Italian vermouth

Combine ingredients in a cocktail shaker half-filled with ice. Shake well and strain into a cocktail glass.

RUMMY SOUR

$1\frac{1}{4}$ ounces spiced rum
$1\frac{3}{4}$ ounces lemon-lime mix

Blend ingredients with a scoop of crushed ice in a blender and serve in a margarita glass.

JACK OF HEARTS (SHOT)

$\frac{1}{3}$ ounce Jägermeister
$\frac{1}{3}$ ounce peach schnapps
$\frac{1}{3}$ ounce cranberry juice

Combine ingredients in a cocktail shaker half-filled with ice. Shake well and strain into a shot glass.